D0501847

Managing with the Wisdom of Love

Dorothy Marcic

Managing with the Wisdom of Love

Uncovering Virtue in People and Organizations

Jossey-Bass Publishers • San Francisco

Copyright © 1997 by Jossey-Bass Inc., Publishers, 350 Sansome Street, San Francisco, California 94104.

All rights reserved. No part of this publication may be reproduced, stored in a retrieval system, or transmitted, in any form or by any means, electronic, mechanical, photocopying, recording, or otherwise, without the prior written permission of the publisher.

The last stanza of "A Basket of Fresh Bread" (page 43) is from J. Rumi, *This Longing,* 1988. Used by permission of Threshold Books, RD 4 Box 600, Putney, VT 05346.

Chapter Three epigraph by Vinson Brown (page 45) is from WARRIORS OF THE RAINBOW by William Willoya and Vinson Brown, Naturegraph Publishers, Happy Camp, CA 96039. Used by permission.

Chapter Four epigraph by Black Elk (page 89) is from BLACK ELK SPEAKS by John G. Neihardt. Used by permission of the University of Nebraska Press.

Substantial discounts on bulk quantities of Jossey-Bass books are available to corporations, professional associations, and other organizations. For details and discount information, contact the special sales department at Jossey-Bass Inc., Publishers (415) 433-1740; Fax (800) 605-2665.

For sales outside the United States, please contact your local Simon & Schuster International Office.

Jossey-Bass Web address: http://www.josseybass.com

 Manufactured in the United States of America on Lyons Falls Turin Book. This paper is acid-free and 100 percent totally chlorine-free.

Library of Congress Cataloging-in-Publication Data

Marcic, Dorothy.
    Managing with the wisdom of love : uncovering virtue in people and organizations / Dorothy Marcic.—1st ed.
        p.   cm.—(The Jossey-Bass business and management series)
    Includes bibliographical references and index (p.   ).
    ISBN 0-7879-0173-3
    1. Management—Religious aspects.   2. Spiritual life.
    3. Interpersonal relations—Religious aspects.   I. Title.
    II. Series.
    HD38.M3234   1997
    658—dc21   97-1668

FIRST EDITION
HB Printing   10 9 8 7 6 5 4 3 2 1

The Jossey-Bass

Business & Management Series

Contents

For Raymond, my brother, whose love has been my guide
For Margaret Clayton, ever steadfast, whose
dignity rises above any tempest or storm
And for William Sears, whose joie de vivre
taught me that God loves laughter

In memory of Jeffrey Mondschein
1952–1996

Preface

As a management consultant and professor for more than twenty years, I have struggled to make sense of complex and troubling organizational problems and crises, many of which have seemed impervious to change. Much of these twenty years has been spent trying to figure out why our organizations don't work better.

What I have often seen is well-meaning managers and employees who end up angry, hurt, resentful, and demotivated. It is too often like a Greek tragedy, in which no one is bad but some "fatal flaws" of character, personality, or style bring about an almost inevitable downfall. Because little learning may result from these misfortunes, they become all the more tragic. No one understands what happened or learns how to prevent similar outcomes in the future. I have come to see that these bewildering problems are rooted at least partially in a lack of awareness of spiritual law and its relevance to the workplace.

The seeds of my own ever-growing awareness of this law were planted nearly three decades ago. I didn't take physics until my second semester of college. I had avoided it in high school, partly because I graduated a year early and partly because all my friends told me it was too hard and a useless subject anyway. But because it was a requirement at the University of Wisconsin, I finally enrolled in a physics class, and almost failed the midterm exam. My friends were right, I thought. It is hard, it is stupid.

But then something happened. I started to get it. The magic of the laws of the universe made sense to me. It was all so incredibly fascinating, captivating, and fun. I was in love. For the first time in my life I was head over heels in love with a subject.

Then I became angry at all of the people who had steered me clear of this new world. How could they have been so wrong? How could I have been so misled? How could I have so easily believed them? And my math teachers, too. Why hadn't they told me that learning equations was for a reason, a very wonderful reason?

Studying physics changed my life. I was never the same again. The mysteries of the world around me began to change into a marvelous structure. What had been invisible was now clear. Finally I understood what gravity was all about, why a ball goes in an arc when you throw it, what happens with mass and velocity. The fact that I had not understood these laws previously, and had even avoided that understanding, had not made them inoperative for me. I had been subject to them the same as everyone else. Whether I knew these principles or not, I couldn't throw a baseball any faster than the laws of physics allowed.

At about the same time that I discovered physics I also began a spiritual quest that continues to this day. And just as with physics, this spiritual journey has changed my life in many ways. For example, one thing I have learned on this journey that is similar to my early insights in physics is that we live in a world governed by law—in this case, spiritual law—which is often presented in the form of precepts or commands, such as "Thou shalt be honest," "Thou shalt treat others with dignity," and "Thou shalt live in justice." And breaking spiritual law, whether in business or not, has certain predictable results.

Once again I am discovering a path that others may see as worthless, irrelevant, or too difficult. But while these insights are more exciting than my first insights in physics, ultimately they are as practical and applicable. This path has shown me the importance of spiritual law and its relation to love and virtue, and this book is about these three.[1]

I wrote this book for managers who are trying to figure out why their elaborately planned programs don't work, why morale is low or trust is absent, or why worker motivation just isn't what it ought to be, and for anyone who realizes that scientific formulas and materialistic solutions are not the complete answer to organizational problems. My hope is that together we may search beyond our inadequacies to understand what we could be and the kind of organizations we could create.

Contents

In the prelude, I discuss the nature of love and spirituality. Chapter One presents the need for love in the workplace. Because the "balance" of love with the physical and intellectual dimensions of an organization is important, a model of the organization as a tree is explained in Chapter Two. Chapter Three describes the new management virtues, which grow out of spiritual law and which many companies are practicing. Several companies using these new virtues are highlighted in Chapter Four. Finally, Chapter Five provides suggestions for how to operationalize spirituality and the new management virtues in the workplace.

Acknowledgments

The writing of this book has been a labor of love—not only *from* me, out of my love for the material, but also *for* me, from so many people whose love and support have been precious to me. First, I wish to thank Herman Poort, who served as my assistant on this book for more than a year. He helped with research, permissions, editing, and general bouncing around of ideas. Without Herman's help I would not have come so far in the time allowed. Other people who helped immensely with intellectual, spiritual, material, and emotional support include Farhad Fozdar (whose generosity was a blessing), Peter Vaill (who challenged and encouraged me at many stages), Stephen and Nadjla Birkland (whose prayers and conceptual help were appreciated), Michal Cakrt (my close colleague for four years in the Czech Republic), Petr Trmac (whose tireless library research was immensely useful), Roman Bohacek, Patricia Hampl (my friend and colleague from Minnesota and, later, Prague), Pauline Barnes, Joe Mestenhauser, Wendy Momen (whose un-bounded enthusiasm was an inspiration to me), Farhad Pimoradi, Rose Presser, Marketa Glancova, Jan Orlik, Susan Herman, Serge Thill, Greg Dahl, Mark Kriger, Becky Buckosh, Lisa Rosenblate, Ezzat Zahrai, Venus Ferdowski, Howie Schwartz, and Ernie Kurtz. Deans I served under while writing the book were Bill Pendergast and Josephine Olson, both of whom gave me ample support. I want to thank administrators of the Fulbright Scholar program in the Czech Republic and Washington, D. C., including Vaclav Aschen-brenner, Hanna Ripkova, Marilyn Wyatt, Leslie High, and espe-cially Ambassador Adrian Basora, who helped my light to shine. Much of this book was written during the three years I spent as a Fulbright Scholar in Prague. Diane Casbolt Garga continually gave me ideas, while Dick Bauman provided me with important insights on authority. I am grateful also to Jeffrey Mondschein for steering me in the direction of ServiceMaster, and to George Starcher, who offered me many resources and made available to me his incredible network in Europe and the United States. And I could not have completed this project as I wanted without the generous help of Susan Maneck, Vahid Behmardi, and Moojan Momen, widely rec-ognized religious scholars, who shared ideas, feedback, and scrip-tures with me.

During the time this book was being written, several dear friends died. They all touched my life in different ways, offering love and encouragement at various times of my life. My sympathy goes to the families of Jerry and Patty Boisclair, Jeffrey Mondschein, and Clifford Gray.

At Jossey-Bass I was encouraged, listened to, and guided by William Hicks and more recently by Byron Schneider and Cedric Crocker for almost two years since the first proposal. Their love and support kept me going through some difficult times. Byron, in fact, became a champion for the book, keeping it and me on the right track. Jan Hunter offered important developmental support. And during the final stages, Maggie Stuckey and Mary Garrett were key in giving the book a sharp focus.

On the home front, I could not have managed as a single mother to three daughters without my housekeeper, Marie Miller, the mother of my friend Ludek Miller. Marie kept us all sane when I felt I might go in the other direction. Then there was my friend Maja Curhova, who with love helped me with my children.

Which brings me to my family and my daughters, Roxanne, Solange, and Elizabeth, who showed much patience while I was working on the manuscript, often doing their homework on the floor next to the computer where I was writing. Solange helped me by providing a quote from *Chicken Soup for the Soul* (Canfield and Hansen, 1993), one of her favorite books. I hope the experience of writing about love has taught me how to be a better mother. My sister, Janet Mittelsteadt, went through a tough battle with cancer while I was writing this book and helped me to see another depth of love. I am convinced that all the prayers said around the world by many friends helped to save her. Finally, I must with all my heart thank Richard Daft, who has given his love and encouragement to me, especially in the last stages of the writing, when stress was high and patience low. After I sent the almost final version of the manuscript off to Jossey-Bass, I flew to London, where Dick and I were married. We are beginning a new life together in Nashville, a life filled with hope and love.

February 1997   Dorothy Marcic
Nashville, Tennessee

Managing with the Wisdom of Love

Prelude: A Plea for Love

❧

There is a Law that man should love his neighbor
as himself. In a few years it should be as natural to
mankind as breathing or the upright gait; but if he
does not learn it he must perish.

—*Alfred Adler*

It is the soul of man which first has to be fed.

—*Shoghi Effendi Rabbani*

An ancient Muslim tradition tries to define spirituality by "explaining the smell of a rose." Some say it is impossible. We all know what the aroma is and how we react to it, but put it into words? That is another matter. Similarly, love and spirituality are concepts that transcend the limits of the sensory world, and no matter what we do we end up confining them in a material-world-based language.

The language of science, on which we rely for so much of our modern technology and information, does a wonderful job of defining and measuring the material world, but it cannot achieve the same with the world of spirit or love. For example, I know my husband loves me, but I cannot "prove" or measure it scientifically. Yet I am certain of it at a deep level. Nor can I put my certainty into words that explain or measure that love. For the same reason, I hope the reader will understand that, given the limitations of language, my efforts to write about spirituality and love can only be imperfect.

1

Spirituality, by definition, addresses the world of spirit, the soul, and the sacred. It is a world we cannot see or measure—the non-material world—but it is around us just the same.[1] Spirituality is our means of connecting with that other world, and it is fostered by certain beliefs, attitudes, and behaviors. We see indications of our spiritual development in our relationship with the material world—for instance, in how we treat other people and the environment, as well as in our attitude toward work.

To develop spiritually, we must believe in a dimension of reality beyond what we see and experience as the material world. The evidence of this condition can be as clear as the music of a wind chime. Still, many of us struggle mightily with the notion of believing in and understanding something we cannot see. Perhaps we can better understand spirituality by understanding the nature of spiritual laws, which operate not unlike physical laws, such as gravity.

Spiritual Law

I have no idea how airplanes fly. But they do, whether I understand it or not.

As a management consultant for the past two decades, I have flown frequently, criss-crossing the country and nearly circumnavigating the globe. Every time I fly I wonder how this huge aircraft, weighing hundreds of tons, can possibly be lifted off the ground. It makes absolutely no sense to me how such a mammoth object can, merely by moving faster and faster, suddenly become airborne. Not one to trust lightly, I have asked for insight from engineers and those familiar with aeronautical principles. Even after listening to their lectures and trying to discern the meaning of the simplified diagrams they have drawn for me, I still don't get it. Any comprehensions I might have from physics do not seem to transfer over to my understanding of aeronautics. When I mention this to other people, many say they experience the same syndrome as me. None of us understands, even to the smallest degree, how a vehicle weighing hundreds of tons can rise up and move through the sky. Yet it does somehow, and I, along with others, continue buying airline tickets and flying all around the globe, trusting with our very lives that the incomprehensible principles of aerodynamics will work as we are told they will. It comes down to faith in something I cannot understand or explain.

It is my belief that the world we live in is governed not only by physical laws but also by spiritual ones. Just as my lack of aeronautical intelligence does not change in any way the physical laws that allow airplanes to fly, so it is with spiritual laws. Whether we accept these spiritual laws or not makes no difference in terms of their power or relevance to us. Even if we don't understand or "get it," they still work their wonders on us.

Many Religions, One Message

The spiritual laws that govern human behavior have been articulated for thousands of years by all the world's religions and schools of philosophy, with remarkable consistency. Exhibit P.1 illustrates a few of these laws with quotes from a number of religions. We have been given this ancient wisdom, these precepts for right living and for creating healthy societies, by all of the great religious leaders. The phrasing may be different, but the message is essentially the same: love your neighbor, be honest, live in justice, control your impulses, avoid corruption, let your intentions be pure, and serve your fellow humans.

If religious leaders have been conveying this message in every age, from thousands of years ago to the present, there must be something to all of these instructions. There must be important guidance in them for all of us.

The Wisdom of Love

At the core of all these guiding principles is one fundamental law from which all others spring: love your neighbor and treat your

Exhibit P.1. A Sample of Spiritual Laws from the World's Religions.

Law	Religious Foundation
Be trustworthy	Thou shalt not bear false against thy neighbor. (*Christian, The Bible, Exodus 20:16*)
	The gift of truth excels all gifts. (*Buddhist, Dhammapada 354, 1973*)
	But in torment the soul of the liar shall surely be. (*Zoroastrian, Gathas: Yasna 45:7*, in Mehr, 1991, p. 99)
Be detached, remove ego	. . . give up pride. (*Buddhist, Dhammapada 221*)
Do not live in anger	Absence of anger, . . . indignation [and] of enmity; [this is] approved conduct for men in all stations of life. (*Hindu, Apastamba Dharma Sutra, 8:1*, in Morgan, 1953, pp. 324–325)
Live in service	For the sake of the welfare of all, carry on thy task in life. (*Hindu, The Bhagavad Gita, 3:20*, 1984, p. 58)
	Again, is there any deed in the world that would be nobler than service to the common good? This is worship: to serve mankind. (*Bahá'í*, in *Paris Talks* by 'Abdu'l-Bahá, p. 177)
Love others	Hate is not conquered by hate. Hate is conquered by love. This is an eternal law. (*Buddhist, Dhammapada 5, 1973*)
	. . . love your enemies, bless them that curse you . . . love thy neighbor as thyself. (*Christian, The Bible, Matthew 5:44, 19:19*)

neighbor as you would wish to be treated. Although not all religious texts use the word *love* to portray this principle, in fact love is the common thread underlying all spiritual laws. From this precept, which we can call "the Wisdom of Love," derive all the laws of honorable living.

By following these spiritual laws, we develop our spiritual natures and acquire virtues, such as trustworthiness, respect, patience, and so on. Virtues become, then, the outward manifestation of our inward spirituality, which is rooted in love.

When asked what was the most important commandment, Jesus replied that it was to love God with all your heart and soul, and the second was to "love your neighbor as yourself. There is no commandment greater than these" (Mark 12: 29–31). This commandment has been so important that it has been termed "the Golden Rule."[2] In fact, though many people in Western societies associate this principle with Jesus, the concept itself actually preceded him and has been an integral part of all the major religions. It goes as far back as early Judaism, Hinduism, and Buddhism, and ancient Zoroastrianism, as evidenced by the following excerpts from their literature (the dates are the approximate beginnings of the religions):[3]

Judaism (c. fourteenth century B.C.)[4]

A certain unbeliever came to Rabbi Shammai and said: "Convert me provided that you teach me the entire Torah while I stand on one foot." Shammai drove away the inquirer with the builder's cubit which was in his hand, and went to Rabbi Hillel who said: "What is hateful to you, do not do to your neighbor; that is the entire Torah; the rest is commentary; go learn it."

—*Babylonian Talmud*, Shabbat 31a
(cited in Glatzer, 1969, p. 197)

Hinduism (Vedic religion from c. thirteenth century B.C.; Upanishads from fifth century B.C.)

Do not to others what ye do not wish done to yourself. This is the whole Dharma; heed it well.

> —*The Mahābhārata* (cited in Das, 1995, p. 398)

Zoroastrianism (c. twelfth century B.C.)[5]

Human nature is good only when it does not do unto another whatever is not good for its own self.

> —*Dādistān-ī-Dīnīk*, 94:5 (cited in Müller, Chapter 94, Vol. 18, 1882, p. 269)

Buddhism (c. sixth century B.C.)

Hurt not others in ways that you yourself would find hurtful.

> —*Udānavarga*, 5:18 (cited in Tibetan Dhammapada, 1986)

Jainism (c. sixth century B.C.)

In happiness and suffering, in joy and grief, regard all creatures as you would regard your own self.

> —*Yoga-Śāstra* (cited in Bull, 1969, p. 92)

Confucianism (c. sixth century B.C.)

Do not do to others what you do not want done to yourself.

> —Confucius, *The Analects*, 15:23, 6:28; Mahabharara, 5:1517 (cited in Confucius, *The Analects*, 1992)

Christianity (c. first century A.D.)

Do unto others as you would have them do unto you.

—Jesus Christ, *The Bible*, Luke 6:13

Islam (c. seventh century A.D.)

No one of you is a believer until you desire for another that which you desire for yourself.

—*The Sunnah* (from the Ḥadīth)

Sikhism (c. fifteenth century A.D.)

Be not estranged from another for, in every heart, Pervades the Lord.

—Sri Guru Granth Sahib (cited in Singh, 1963, p. 250)

Baha'i (c. nineteenth century A.D.)

Ascribe not to any soul that which thou wouldst not have ascribed to thee, and say not that which thou doest not. This is my command unto thee, do thou observe it.

—Bahá'u'lláh, *Hidden Words*, Arabic 29

What Goes Around Comes Around

Just as appreciating the physical laws of the universe helps us to conceptualize the spiritual laws, it also teaches us the notion of consequences—that certain actions lead to predictable reactions. The idea of there being consequences to action for material objects was conceptualized by Isaac Newton in the seventeenth century. For example, when a ball with a certain mass is thrown at a particular angle, the arc at which it travels can be determined mathematically.

Spiritual laws also have consequences, and whether we are aware of spiritual law or not, we are still subject to those consequences. The consequences are not always as obvious as a falling apple, particularly if we do not wish to see them, and often they are not as immediate. In the short term, we may ignore spiritual laws with impunity, but eventually the consequences of our actions will become manifest.

For instance, if I decide to live my life according to the basic spiritual law of loving my neighbor, one thing that means is that I must be honest in my dealings with people. If I obey the law of honesty, it means I will treat others with integrity and reliability. As a result, most people over time will trust me and this trust will serve to enhance my relationships with them. However, if I decide to defy this spiritual law and lie to others, try to cheat them clandestinely, or not do what I had promised, after a while they will not trust me and will tend to avoid me if they have a choice.

Whether I "believe" in honesty is of no consequence. Once a behavior causes trust to be broken, it doesn't matter whether either party understands that the spiritual law of honesty was broken— the net result is still loss of trust.

Of course, when it comes to human interaction there may be several factors at work, and it may be difficult to see the separate consequences of each factor. On any given day, an individual is subject to many forces that shape behavior, and not all of them are in response to the actions of others. In general, however, we can proceed through life knowing that following the law of honesty builds trustworthiness, and that without question, breaking that law destroys trust.

Love and Action

Love and spirituality are about transformation. The quest for spirituality and the sacred is a process that requires honest and reflective self-evaluation. It obligates change. Change is a process of moving closer and closer to a more virtuous state. Having "faith" or feeling "connected" with others without any changes to the inner self or outward action is not true spirituality but rather the form without the content.[6] It would be like an organization claiming to adopt a more Japanese style of management while only appointing a few quality circle groups with little authority or input. Similarly, a manager or consultant who institutes a "spirituality program" without going through the necessary personal changes cannot expect anything more than a superficial outcome.

Our behaviors are an outward manifestation of our inner life. If others cannot discern indications of our spirituality in our behavior, then it is not likely to be evident within ourselves either. Some people think that spirituality and daily practical life are separate issues. One of the purposes of this book is to show that spiritual behaviors should be practiced in a factory as much as in a temple.

Loving *feelings* toward your neighbor are not in themselves sufficient. Real love requires action, and the willingness to stretch yourself in order to nurture another's growth.

> My little children, let us not love in word, neither in tongue; but in deed and in truth.
>
> —Christian, The Bible, 1 John 3:18

Real love is operationalized through virtuous behavior. This behavior can become a *force*, a power in itself. Just as peace is not merely the absence of war (as we are witnessing since the fall of the Soviet empire) but instead a force that must be nurtured on its own, so is love a force. Love is manifest as an intention for betterment, which is usually revealed in a positive result.

By loving someone, we can actually foster that person's development. Our love serves as a catalyst to that person's growth.[7] By believing and having faith in others, we help them to increase their self-esteem and their faith in themselves, which increases their energy and desire to become more than they are now.

Love and Spirituality in the Workplace

The Wisdom of Love precept that guides us on the path for right living on a personal level also shows us the way to create healthy organizations. Business exists in the same physical and spiritual world as every other unit of society and is dependent on the same physical and spiritual laws. There are not two sets of spiritual laws, one for everyday life and another for business; there is only one. Whether managers want to see this or not is irrelevant. The same laws apply to them as to everyone else, even when they are ignorant of them. Ideas in the Tao are similar: "Natural law is blind, its justice evenhanded. The consequences of one's behavior are inescapable" (Heider, 1985, p. 9).

This book is about taking a journey and finding out what these spiritual laws are and figuring out what they mean for businesses and for managers. My premises are that these spiritual laws exist and that we have been given wisdom throughout the ages on how to follow these laws in order to, as a result, develop virtuous behavior. I invite you on this journey with me to explore why spiritual law and the management virtues that flow from it are relevant for modern business.

Part of our journey will be to better understand what love is and what it means in the workplace. Some say love has no place at work. I don't think we have a choice on that one, however. Love has its own laws. Just as the law of honesty operates both inside and outside of business, so does the power of love. We may choose to deny it, ignore it, or abuse it, but it is still there, and we will still live the consequences of how we use the force of love.

> *And though I . . . understand all mysteries, and all knowledge; and though I have all faith, so that I could remove mountains, and have not love, I am nothing.*
>
> —Christian, *The Bible*, 1 Corinthians 13:2

The day will come when after harnessing space, the winds, the tides and gravitation, we shall harness for God the energies of love. And on that day, for the second time in the history of the world, we shall have discovered fire.

—Teilhard de Chardin[8]

Chapter One

Spirituality in the Workplace

❧

Good management is largely a matter of love . . .
because proper management involves caring for
people, not manipulating them.
> —*James A. Autry*, Love and Profit

Love is ever the beginning of Knowledge as fire is
of light.
> —*J. W. von Goethe*

When is the last time you heard the world *love* spoken at your place of work? *Love* is rarely used in the same sentence with the words *business* or *management*. Mention love in a business meeting and you'll likely get either glazed-over eyes or teenage locker-room banter. We'd have a hard time finding the word *love* in many company policy manuals or in management textbooks. The closest words you might find are *empathy* (in listening), *positive reinforcement* (in behavior management), or *cohesion* (in group development), all of which may be components of love but are not the whole thing.

Most of us would find it suffocating to even think of living without love. How is it that the glue that holds together our families and other important relationships seems to be absent in the organizational world?

About ten years ago I thought that because most of us come out of dysfunctional families, we later create dysfunctional organizations. At that time others were writing about similar themes. One of my favorites back then was Roger Evered and Jim Selman's

(1988) article "Managers Anonymous." They hypothesized that managers suffer from the disease of "managerism," which is an addiction to nonproductive behaviors even in the face of data showing the dire consequences of these behaviors. Then there was J. B. Ritchie of Brigham Young University, whose goal was to teach students to protect themselves from pervasive "organizational abuse" (1984).

These days I see the basic problem differently. In my search to understand what has been happening in organizations, I began to see that dysfunctional managers are not the causal factor, as I had previously thought, but symptoms of some deeper problem. The root cause is lack of love. The problems that we are seeing in dysfunctional organizations are merely symptoms of lovelessness and negligence of spiritual law.

Staying clear on the true cause of the problem will get us pointed in the right direction toward its solution. The foundation of the ills of modern organizations cannot be solved by sending managers to more training programs, by hiring more Harvard MBAs, by "doing TQM," by developing a comprehensive and cutting-edge strategy, or even by installing a "spirituality" program. Certainly these tactics may be important and useful ingredients in the continuous improvement of an organization. They are not, however, the real solutions, the actions that will bring long-term health. What modern organizations need is a moral foundation, an infusion of spirituality, a recognition that a fundamental source of our problems is lack of love.

Spirituality and the Wisdom of Love

Why all this talk of love in business organizations? Because the power of love and of spiritual law operate with the same inexorability inside business organizations as outside them.

Unfortunately, managers and those who write about management have neglected to remember this simple principle: we inhabit the same physical and spiritual space as other members and systems of this world, and are subject to the same laws and the same consequences of those laws.

What would it mean if we would love our subordinates, our bosses, and our colleagues as ourselves? It would mean we would not intentionally hurt them, we wouldn't treat them unjustly, and we would act towards them with dignity and respect.[1] Such are some of the building blocks of a healthy and thriving system. It doesn't matter whether you use *love* or some other word to describe these behaviors; if you treat all the people you work with the way you would like to be treated, then you are in fact operating through the Wisdom of Love. And if all the executives and managers of the organization are guided by this principle in the decisions they make, then we can say that the organization, the cumulative entity, has spirituality as at least part of its foundation.

New Values for Managers

Most MBA or management training programs don't teach future managers to love their employees or customers, or to create an environment in which love can thrive. Until quite recently, the largely unquestioned maxims for managers were variations of the following: Be in charge! Control resources and people (who are part of the resources)! Plan your work and work your plan! Be a tough-minded manager! Maintain discipline! Get them to do what you want them to do!

Managers are urged toward all this toughmindedness, and at the same time are expected to develop high-performing teams, which need to be empowered, to be listened to, and to have their social needs fulfilled in order to achieve the desired levels of performance (Peters, 1987; Schmidt and Finnigan, 1992; Nadler and Gerstein, 1992). Peak performers describe their state as being energized, enthusiastic, focused, confident, and so on. They say that such characteristics result from commitment on their part as well as from challenge and a sense of purpose (Adams, 1984b). These positive qualities are rarely found in work groups that are based on self-centered and self-aggrandizing motives, or in environments of distrust, suspicion, and intrigue. Organizations wanting high commitment from workers can get it only if they sincerely value the contributions of workers and create a trusting atmosphere (Green and Hatch, 1990). These attitudes form part of the aggregate of loving behaviors. They represent the Wisdom of Love in action.

What we are talking about here is love operationalized as community-building in organizations. When we do apparent good deeds but do them with the intention of some sort of reward or recognition or out of fear of punishment, then we are doing them for a self-centered motive, even though the behavior may be helpful to others (Jackall, 1988). However, if we do those same actions but with the purpose of bettering the group, then we can truly experience "community."[2]

Without love there can be no sense of community. Managers who are concerned mostly with their own welfare, with their own needs being met, cannot be outstanding managers and will not create a long-term, outstanding organization. To accomplish sustainable success, managers must sincerely care for the needs of others, helping them in selfless ways, the ways that build community. In this vein, one successful executive's bumper sticker of choice would be "If you're not creating community, you're not managing" (Autry, 1991, p. 145).

Consequences of Breaking Spiritual Laws

Companies that break spiritual laws, that lack love, integrity, justice, and respect, will over time show negative effects in some way. They may be initially successful, or even successful for quite a while, particularly if they have clever managers or little competition. However, the results of lovelessness, injustice, and disrespect will eventually make the organization less productive than it might have been. In the long run, the company will suffer alienation of workers, disenfranchisement of customers, loss of community respect, and so on.

Early Zoroastrianism had a well-defined law of consequences, the law of *Asha* (similar to the Hindu *dharma* and Buddhist *dhamma*), which indicates that all people receive the fruit of their own actions—or *Mizdem* (akin to *karma* in Buddhism and Hinduism) (Mehr, 1991). This ancient teaching recognizes the positive potential of our behaviors as well as the darker side of human nature, the capacity to behave either honorably or despicably. In the case of managers, the choice is between using power for the good of the organization and people, and abusing that power.

Companies that follow rather than break spiritual laws will be the long-term winners. Many elements contribute to a company's success—correct anticipation of consumer demand, cost efficiencies in manufacturing and distribution, increased productivity, design innovations, and swift adaptation to market changes. In today's competitive environment, businesses have to do everything right; failure in any of these areas can mean bankruptcy. Positive outcomes are not always automatic, or obvious.

This is not a book about marketing, or productivity, or strategic planning per se. It is about spirituality. It is about conducting business from a spiritual base, in whatever circumstances the company happens to find itself, and seeing the positive effect of spirituality ripple throughout the rest of the organization—including the marketing, productivity, and strategic planning functions.

One positive outcome of following spiritual laws is seeing success in broader terms than simply an increase in profits. It is important to emphasize that following spiritual laws simply with the hope of becoming more profitable breaks the law of purity of motive and tends to somewhat neutralize the effects of the effort.[3] Purity of motive means a manager would work toward virtuous behavior without expectation of reward. Whether a reward is received, then, has no influence on the choice to be virtuous again. Without purity of motive, an executive is likely to "try spirituality" but quickly lose interest if the bottom line does not see quick improvement.

In general I believe that "right living" can have very positive empirical results. Chapter Four includes the stories of many business organizations whose success testifies to this truth. For now, those of you who are persuaded by numbers might consider this: a joint European-American study of three thousand strategic units showed much higher return on investment (ROI) for units practicing good human relations policies, such as justice in compensation, reduction of conflict, encouragement of a sense of accomplishment, participation in decisions, information sharing, creation of feelings of belonging, and openness to change. The impact of such policies was much greater for companies in unstable environments (unpredictable changes in markets, competition, and technology), which showed +16.7 percent higher ROI, than for those in stable environments, which showed +3.8 percent ROI (Mack, 1992).

Sociologist James Coleman argues that love increases not only economic well-being, as exemplified in the study just discussed, but also nearly every other element of social existence (Fukuyama, 1995, p. 10). It creates a tremendous resource of *social capital,* the capacity of people to subordinate individual interests and work together in groups for common purposes. Without love, there can be no group commitment and therefore no social capital.

Learning to Love

If all this is so important, so obvious, why are we not applying the force of love more? Why aren't we learning better how to love? I believe that most of us working with organizations truly want to be more effective, but we haven't yet figured out some of these basic principles of operating with other humans. Instead, we try this and that, and later stand confused, wondering why the outcome wasn't as good as we expected.

The key, I believe, is that we are not looking in the right place. We expend most of our efforts on the company's physical and intellectual dimensions (see Chapter Two), and almost none on the spiritual. The things we try will not succeed unless they address the organization's spiritual core, and unless our efforts themselves are based in loving behaviors. This is crucial: as we work to improve the organization's spiritual dimension, we must make sure that in the process we do not violate spiritual law.

Management consultants are as guilty as anyone else. We go into organizations with our formulas, strategies, and overwhelming information. Yet without love, these tools cannot be used to their fullest potential and may even inflict harm. A loveless organization has selfishness, political infighting, petty jealousies, lies, and distrust. What good is the most advanced, cutting-edge information system if it is used to withhold facts from certain groups, to give some people advantage over others, or to convey a false reality to employees? And how helpful is yet another management training program about communication, diversity, and empowerment if it only adds to a manager's repertoire of manipulations? "Only basic goodness gives life to technique" (Covey, 1989a).

Some organizations, believing they are on the right track at last, institute programs in spirituality or community building, only to have them fall flat. Then the managers can say, "See I told you spirituality won't work!" True, it will not "work" if it is anything less than authentic and does not deal with the core values of the organization. People are not stupid. In the many years I have worked with organizations, I have been continually impressed with the insight and awareness of many employees, and especially of many work groups. Sometimes these people sense intentions that are less than pure, or programs that have been designed to make them feel good without doing much to change any structural injustices or to improve honest communication. Initially they may appreciate the efforts for change, but when nothing really changes, over time they become resentful, angry, and alienated. After a while, management realizes that there are new problems (actually just the same ones revisited) and calls for another program. With each new and redesigned but finally ineffective program, workers become increasingly cynical. "Oh, not another consultant!" they say.

My daughter taught me a stunning lesson in authenticity at Sunday brunch not long ago. We lived for four years in Prague, where I was teaching, and my children adopted many European customs. On this particular Sunday, I was trying my best to get Elizabeth, who was then eight, to use her utensils "properly," instead of using the odd and clumsy combination of American and European techniques she fancied. She became frustrated at my repeated corrections, and I became frustrated at her resistance. Finally, hoping to win her with logic, I pleaded, "But I am only trying to be helpful!"

She just looked at me. Seeing through my hypocritical intentions with a child's clear insight, she protested, "That's not helpful, it's worseful!"

Since that day, I have meditated on the wisdom of a child many times. How often we do things with the assumption that it is helping when it fact it is "worseful." Managers are as big a culprit as parents.

We in the management profession have marched forth with statistics, formulas, quotients, and strategies, in the name of productivity and with the intention of being helpful. Statistics and formulas can be most helpful, but without an equal concern for the human element, we have helped erode some important community values. Applying changes that break spiritual laws results in a "worseful" ending. I can just hear my daughter shouting from the back of the room at a professional conference where someone is describing some new "system" that will revolutionize the workplace and how much it will help productivity: "That's not helpful, it's worseful!"

Spiritual Motives

What we are about here is strengthening the organization's spiritual dimension, putting the business on a firm foundation of ethics, integrity, and honor. Although everything I have learned about organizations, including the experiences of the companies you will read about later in this book, leaves no doubt that spiritual companies can be profitable companies, I do not propose that any organization proceed from that motivation alone. I believe, quite simply, that they should do it because it is the right thing to do.

When the overarching goal of the organization is only profit and the increase of shareholder wealth, it is difficult to create a spiritual framework, for as soon as the bottom line is threatened, love goes out the window as an expendable commodity. In such an environment, everyone is geared toward the profit goals and tries to "fit in" spirituality. For love and spirituality to really work, however, the profit goals must be partners with spiritual goals, such as contributing to the community, developing employees, or creating community within the organization.

> *Devote thyself to My service, do all thine acts for My sake, and thou shalt attain the goal.*
>
> —Hindu, *Bhagavad-Gita*, 12:10
> (cited in *The Geeta*, 1986)

The spiritual motive is all the more significant because of what has been occurring in business worldwide. As Willis Harman and John Hormann (1990) have reminded us, business is in a critical position at this point in history. Because the influence of governments and religious organizations has seriously eroded, they offer little hope to troubled societies for overcoming the previously unimaginable and complex problems afflicting much of the world. Perhaps only business has the resources, competence, and credibility to begin to tackle these predicaments. Large multinational corporations have bigger budgets than many of the world's countries. Also, trading across borders helps create a kind of unity that often supersedes anything politics can offer. Larry Miller once commented, "Doing business with other countries creates new partners, and who is going to want to shoot the partner?" (personal communication, January 1986).

International business dealings and the resultant publicity have helped to bring into the light of day gross abuses in factories. Increases in the off-shore manufacture of clothing resulted in a lot of press and public outcry about sweatshop conditions in parts of

Asia. Motivated by either high social goals or savvy public relations advice, several companies hired inspectors and quit subcontracting manufacturing out to the sweatshops; as a result, these companies may ultimately be a force for positive social change. A few years ago such behavior by a U.S. multinational would have been almost unthinkable, but offshore reliance has increased and media has focused attention on harsh conditions. A growing list of companies, including Wal-Mart Stores, Nordstrom, Levi Strauss & Co., and Reebok International, are developing standards for hired factories from wage levels to workers' rights to safety. An official at the International Labor Organization, a United Nations agency in Geneva, says, "It is a healthy development that helps employers see that humane treatment won't bankrupt a company" (Zachary, 1994, p. 1).

With the incredible resources that business commands, if it also has lofty social goals whose underlying forces are spiritual and if it works toward the development of virtues, it can be the most effective means for creating a better life for billions of people.

The proper man understands equity, the small man profits.

—Confucius (cited in Seldes, 1985)

Spirituality Is a Process, Not a Product

Each year or so a new fad emerges on the management scene and many people become rich giving seminars or writing books. My fear is that spirituality has already been relegated to this novelty-of-the-month status. In the process, true spirituality has been marginalized. It is now a popular word, an interesting concept, and many are using it to gain attention, popularity, or monetary reward.

Some of the current discussions on spirituality have little depth to them. Spirituality has become, to some, an amusement. What a pity if the real message gets lost in techniques, buzzwords, and new dogmas. Spirituality is not something we can really grasp merely by reading books (including this one) or by getting into long, involved discussions. Instead, it requires becoming involved in the process itself.

> A *virtuous life requires exertion, and does not consist in amusement.*
>
> —Aristotle (as cited in Seldes, 1985, p. 18)

Can an organization be spiritual? If its members work on collectively developing virtues and operate with "right views, right aspirations" (from Buddha's Eightfold path, as cited in Fozdar, 1973, p. 46), and so on, is it in fact spiritual? Perhaps—at the moment.

Spiritual development is all process, all movement. We can never say we have arrived. A determination that Company A is spiritual is meaningless. All we can acknowledge is that *at this point in time* Company A is on a spiritual path and has adopted some processes or programs based on developing certain virtues.

We cannot give any "spirituality awards" to companies; we can only look at an organization's attempts at growth on this path. Anyone or any organization can and will backslide. The point, though, is not to be discouraged, but to once more move ahead. It is not *where* you are that counts, but whether you are *moving forward.*

Chapter Two

Moving Toward Balance

*If I had my life to live over again, I would have
made it a rule to read some poetry and listen to
some music at least once a week; for perhaps the
parts of my brain now atrophied would have thus
been kept active through use. The loss of these
tastes is a loss of happiness, and may possibly be
injurious to the intellect, and more probably to the
moral character, by enfeebling the emotional part
of our nature.*

—*Charles Darwin*

The life of most modern managers is filled with confusion, uncertainty, and anxiety. Many problems in their organizations remain unsolved or are made worse by lack of understanding of the problem's causes. I cannot begin to describe all the organizational traumas I have seen that resulted from management's inability or unwillingness to examine the underlying dynamics of the situation and apply relevant management principles. It was either "business as usual," even if the typical way did not work, or if some attempt at a new approach was made, it was often a half-hearted "program of the month." In the end, no one really learned anything, and without additional understanding, organizations are doomed to repeat the cycle all over again.

The many problems I have seen during almost twenty years of teaching management and providing management consulting can be conveniently divided into a few categories: the increasing greed of business; ethical violations; lack of sensitivity to workers' needs, as evidenced by outrageous CEO salaries and massive layoffs of hundreds of thousands of workers; intensifying hucksterism in the marketplace; and worker oppression.[1] These problems are for the most part indications of a spiritual crisis. Witness the following examples that I have seen or heard about in my work with organizations:

- An organization in which the most challenging problem of more than half the employees was "making it through until retirement." It's not hard to imagine the impoverished motivation level of that group.
- Organizations that "strip" jobs from workers and feel no guilt or remorse, and don't try in more than cursory ways to give retribution.
- Employees who feel exploited or humiliated, who in return work less or sabotage results, or steal office supplies, long distance telephone calls, or other resources. They wait patiently for their chance to get back at the organization.
- Employees who expect to be victimized and therefore react in hostile and noncooperative ways to management. Such behavior naturally serves only to distance workers from management and to make management think negatively about employees. It becomes a self-fulfilling prophecy.
- The organization exhibiting "all the ugly manifestations of control, manipulation, dishonesty, withholding information, [and] divide-and-conquer tactics, [where] morale is dismal" and tyranny reigns (Marilyn O'Brien, personal communication, October 1995).
- The employee who for years feels misunderstood, neglected, unappreciated, exploited, and even abused, who one day comes to work with a gun and uses it.

Perhaps the cruelest example—because it promises so much and delivers so little—is the much-vaunted "change" program. It works like this: Management brings in yet another group of consultants to "fix" the problems of poor productivity, lack of communication, and low morale. Everyone is required to attend classes and "motivation sessions." A "restructuring" is proposed. Posters with uplifting slogans that address such issues as positive attitude, appreciation for one another, and honesty are hung up. However, since management rarely follows any of the displayed ideals, after a few months—or weeks—things are back to the way they were, except that now people are more disillusioned than ever.

For many of us, it is not surprising to learn that more than 55 percent of all organizational change efforts fail (Hammer and Champy, 1993). Think what that means: more than half of the time, all the disruption and trauma of change were for naught.

Some critics would argue that the reason these fix-it programs do not succeed is that they go too far into the psychological side of work; they're a waste of money anyway, they say—just get on with business. I disagree. My contention is that often these programs fail because they do not go far enough. The changes tend to be superficial. They do not deal with the core issues of spirit and love, and ultimately do not deliver much. The new organizational scheme is like a rubber band. Stretch it tight and you can hold it in place by brute force; but once the tension for change is gone, the rubber band snaps back in a painful crack.

What is worse, change efforts sometimes derive from less-than-genuine motives. No amount of rhetoric can tune out the intense decibels of managerial hypocrisy or double standards. To be real, to be lasting, change must be genuine and must spring from the deepest, most basic level of human needs and values.

The Five Dimensions of Work

Balance. It's all about balance. Too often we put emphasis on developing our intellectual strength, thereby forgetting our emotional, spiritual, and creative development. When we do this, our greatest strengths become our greatest weaknesses.

This is true for organizations as for individuals. Organizations tend to focus on just one aspect of their nature—their financial well-being, defined quite narrowly.[2] A healthy organization would have a balance of material and physical development, intellectual growth, and a deep concern for human issues.

To look at this balance in organizations, I have built on the models of Peter Vaill (1989), whose organizational components are economic, technological, communal, socio-politico, and moral/spiritual, and on the four agendas in Jack Hawley's (1993) management model of head, heart, body, and spirit, to identify five dimensions of work:

1. *Physical:* concerned with physical life issues, such as buildings, equipment, comfort, safety, and adequate pay.

2. *Intellectual:* includes the collective intelligence of employees plus their continuing drive for further development and learning, as well as abilities to effectively use available resources, to plan productively, and to be on the cutting edge.

3. *Emotional:* involves the interpersonal work environment, how well people get along with each other and how effectively they can be a team. Research shows that effective teams usually need members to be concerned with the *process* skills of support, listening, positive feedback, and lack of defensiveness, all of which require members with mature emotional development.

4. *Volitional:* the desire or will to change for the better. We may know that some other behavior would be healthier but we may lack the will to change it. One psychiatrist wrote that the hardest thing for his patients was not to change but to *decide* to change. Once the will was there, change was relatively easy.

5. *Spiritual:* concerned with moral issues, such as justice and respect, and working toward empathy. Understands each member to be a unique human being, a sacred soul, with dignity.

The model shows the need for any system to be reasonably highly developed in all five dimensions if maximum levels of productivity and effectiveness are desired. All five dimensions are necessary, although well-constructed change programs addressing one or more of those dimensions certainly have a valid role in promoting greater organizational effectiveness in those areas. Many fine books and resources are available to help managers institute a wide variety of change programs. In this book we will concern ourselves with only one dimension—the spiritual—for one simple reason: it is absolutely essential yet largely overlooked in management thinking.

Although we all talk about what has been called "the New Paradigm" (Ray, 1992), it often encompasses only two of the five dimensions. In all study of organizations and how to improve them, most energy is put into focusing on the first two dimensions: the physical, such as work design or conditions, and the intellectual, such as creating challenging work or training people to see jobs or responsibilities differently. Work is, however, also an emotional experience, a concept too often forgotten in management books (Tichy and Sherman, 1993).

A few philosophies of change do address the volitional aspects of work. But virtually none deals with either the emotional or the spiritual aspects. And that, I believe, is the reason so many change efforts fail. The foundation of the problems that change efforts encounter is trustworthiness. People will not truly embrace a change unless they trust those who have created it. Unless people believe that a new initiative is honest, legitimate, and valuable, whatever changes are implemented will not be lasting. The rubber band will snap back, stinging spirits in the process. Without trust, everything else you do is just so much wasted energy.

Trust, personal responsibility, dignity, integrity, and respect—all these issues reside in the organization's *soul*. To address the soul of an organization, we must look particularly at the third and fifth dimensions of work—the emotional and the spiritual. Until we do so, we will continue to find that many of the resources we are pouring into organizational change are indeed wasted.

The Roots of Love

The very idea of focusing on spiritual resources in organizations is startling and confusing to many. For them, I offer the following analogy: the modern organization can be seen as a tree, with roots in the ground and branches reaching out from the trunk and bearing leaves and fruits (see Figure 2.1).

The roots, the part that obtains for the tree its necessary water and nutrients, are the *spiritual* qualities (such as justice, respect, dignity, and the ability to love), which are mostly unseen. They form the foundation of the organization's philosophy, which impacts the entire organization and its policies in such areas as human resource management (fair and equitable recruitment, compensation, and termination programs, as well as respectful negotiation with unions), human resource development (self-managed teams, empowerment, and diversity development programs), ethics (business deals and marketing strategies, and environmental concern), mission statements, values (importance of employees and their development, energy given to being a "good citizen," contribution to arts and social organizations). If the roots are small, weak, or somehow damaged, the tree (the company) cannot receive adequate nourishment and therefore cannot grow to its potential, and it is more vulnerable to environmental traumas such as wind gales, tornadoes, or floods (chaotic economic conditions).

The reach of the tree's roots determines the *volitional* ability of the tree, its willingness to reach out and expand (for organizations, to innovate and adapt), because the deeper and wider spread the roots, the more risks the tree's branches can take. The pervasiveness of the roots' influence is manifested in the flow of vital sustenance throughout the entire tree, in the form of sap, which represents the love and values communicating and uniting with other parts of the tree (organization). Yet the roots and the sap are invisible from normal view.

The *emotional* aspect of the tree is its trunk, which forms the basis of the tree's foundation in the aboveground dimension. Imagine an

Figure 2.1. The Roots of Love in Organizations.

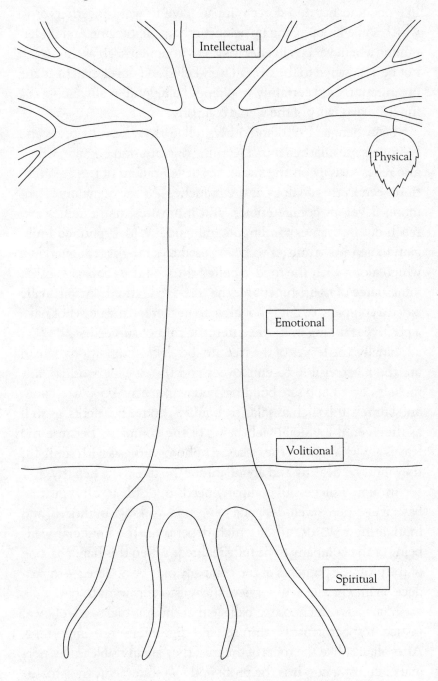

organization with poor social relationships, in which workers don't like one another and don't want to have to work together, or in which some groups gang up against others, sabotaging and undermining whenever possible. A toxic environment such as this would not be conducive to the overall well-being and development of the organization, and certainly would not be helpful in advancing the intellectual quality of the whole company.

Peter Senge (1990) and others tell us that these attitudes and behaviors are anathema to a learning organization climate, which also relies heavily on the *intellectual* development of the organization, seen in this analogy as the branches. As the company learns more, develops competencies, and innovates, its branches can reach out farther, expanding its influence. Wider spanned limbs gain more opportunities to be exposed to sunlight (the market), which along with the food supplied through the roots is another vital source of nourishment for the tree. No matter how spiritually based a company is, if it is not close to its market and does not have a positive standing in it, the enterprise cannot succeed.

Finally, the leaves of the tree are the *physical* conditions, which are the most visible to employees and the outside world. They include decent and safe buildings and workspaces, good work flow, and fair rewards such as salaries, bonuses, and other perks, as well as the overall financial well-being of the company. Because the leaves are what create the necessary photosynthesis with sunlight, they must be healthy and abundant for the tree to be healthy.

In sum, a successful company needs not only a solid spiritual base; it also needs well-designed jobs, good working conditions, and motivating rewards, all of which depend on the financial well-being of the company to be fully realized. When this happens, one of the ultimate purposes of the company may be attained—to produce quality products or services that customers want to buy.

Managers can choose to believe that the spiritual needs of love, justice, respect, trustworthiness, and dignity are not important. After all, just like the roots of the tree, they are invisible under normal circumstances. It is the profit and loss statement, the proverbial bottom line, and the shareholder returns that are considered the truly important issues to attend to.

The abundance and greenness of the leaves are easy to see and measure (the physical dimension), as are the robustness and extension of the branches (the intellectual dimension), so managers know that the health of these two dimensions are essential to the success of the organization. But if the roots are allowed to wither and decay, sooner or later the branches and the leaves also show signs of infirmity, allowing less photosynthesis to take place. Eventually the tree declines and finally dies. Older and larger trees take a longer time for ultimate demise than younger, smaller trees. They live off the accumulated health within the tree, until that is used up, too.

Taking the tree analogy further, the gardener or caretaker of the tree can be considered. Most organizations are begun and developed with some purpose, some thoughtful behavior, in mind. They are not "wild trees," growing accidentally because a seed happened to land in that spot. Instead, many organizations could be considered trees in an orchard, planted with the purpose of bearing some fruit, and perhaps offering beauty as well. Both entrepreneurs as well as managers in older companies are in the position of building up their company and nurturing it, as the gardener or caretaker cares for the orchard. Rather than letting the company grow or die by natural selection, a good manager will purposefully apply methods, techniques, and strategies to make the organization more successful.

The gardener needs to deliberately select the proper nutrients and conditions so the tree not only will survive but will also thrive. These nutrients and conditions might include irrigation (help from bankers or consultants), pesticides (decisive strategies to increase market share), or heat pots during bouts of frost (emergency loans or large doses of caring in times of insecurity). Gardeners also use love and care to nurture their trees. Research with plants has shown that the ones that were talked to and shown love by their caretakers actually grew better (Tart, 1985).

The tree analogy suggests that the organization takes on a life of its own and becomes largely uncontrollable by the manager (the caretaker). What the manager/caretaker can do, though, is create an environment that is more hospitable to the tree's health, or conversely, produce conditions that cause ill health or even demise. By giving proper nutrients to ensure the vigor of the roots (that is, by nurturing spirituality and love as well as volition), the manager/caretaker increases the chances of the tree's ultimate healthy growth.

By ensuring the roots' health, the chances of survival through traumas is increased, too. The deeper the roots go, the more the tree can withstand hurricanes and tornadoes. Organizations that face the turmoils and challenges of market share loss, hazardous competition, product recalls, productivity losses, low innovations, and corrupted executives can, if the roots (love and spirituality) are deep enough, withstand the strongest of challenges.

Even without deep roots, an organization can survive, assuming that no real traumas appear. Or if there are traumas, when the organization is propped up unnaturally (like a tree being held up by steel girders) by trade protection, by governmental shields covering bribes or corruption, or by infusion of government subsidies, it can still survive. There are a number of examples of airline companies being saved from bankruptcy by infusions of government funds. Artificial life supports such as these can cover a multitude of sins for some companies. Under such conditions, however, they will hardly be viable and will not reach their full potential.

Unity is important for the tree to function well. All parts of the tree must have a common purpose. If the trunk and the roots could decide on different rates of growth, the tree would not do as well. Similarly, humility is necessary for the various parts of the tree. The leaves are no more important to the tree than the roots, yet the leaves could make an argument that without them the tree could not use the sunlight. Alternatively, without healthy roots the leaves also could not flourish.

The eye cannot say to the hand, "I have no need of you," nor again the head to the feet, "I have no need of you." On the contrary, the parts of the body which seem to be the weaker are indispensable . . . for if one member suffers, all suffer.

—Christian, 1 Corinthians 13: 21–22,
26

The same is true of the organization as of the tree. All parts must work together in unity, with each unit having a sense of humility toward the other units. Without this, the company cannot prosper.

Companies also cannot survive without sensitivity and a sense of service to the environment. As part of its life, a tree takes in carbon dioxide and gives off oxygen. The ecosystem is dependent on that oxygen, and at the same time on the removal of its carbon dioxide waste by the trees. Thus the tree owes its existence to its interaction with the ecosystem—to its service, in a sense, to the environment. Isn't it the same for a company, which exists as only one part of a symbiotic environment, with each part helping the others?

Interaction of the Five Dimensions

If all five dimensions of work are well developed in an organization, the chances of success and prosperity for that company are quite high. The companies that are most successful over time will tend to be balanced in all five dimensions and will be working to continually improve each one. There is no resting on laurels these days in business.

But what happens when the five are not in harmony? When one or two are developed at the expense of the others? Having any of the five out of balance can be harmful. Some outcomes of such an imbalance are discussed here.

• *Disproportionately developed material dimension.* In this scenario, the owners or managers take advantage of the former success of the company and essentially abuse its resources. They must justify themselves and others by calling the company a "cash cow" that is asking to be "milked." Here the managers are more interested in their own material well-being than in the future well-being of the company or its employees. Since no meaning is gained to meet deeper needs, attempts are made to reduce the resulting emptiness through more and more material progress—better profits and market share, greater salaries and bonuses, increasingly opulent surroundings. This scenario happens sometimes in the third or fourth generation of a successful family business, when the heirs do not have the same commitment to the product or the company as the founders did.

• *Disproportionately developed intellectual dimension.* In such a company, power rests mainly in the hands of the most brilliant minds, especially those who know how to use their expertise to maximize their position in the organization. Intellectual arrogance, and contempt for those perceived as even slightly less fortunate intellectually, is a strong part of the culture. An inordinate amount of time and energy are spent showing up colleagues in competition for the rank of "most brilliant." There is great concern that the company be able to outdo its external competition, but the inner arrogance diminishes the success of those endeavors. This unfortunately seems to be the situation in too many universities, where many professors have developed their intellects at the expense of their social and emotional skills. Brilliant, analytical publications filled with thorough statistical analyses exist here with highly developed minds that judge colleagues by narrow intellectual standards of publication records, rather than using a holistic and human view of total contribution. I have too often seen competent, smart faculty be replaced by arrogant but prolific researchers.

• *Disproportionately developed emotional dimension.* Feeling good, being happy, having interesting work, and being in harmony with coworkers are the most important goals of this type of company. Actual achievement of goals is secondary to happiness. Workers are hyperconcerned about having any tasks that would take too much effort and lead to stress. In this company, coworkers voluntarily spend off-hours together, and there are many company sponsored social events. Sometimes this scenario develops in state-owned companies, where productivity goals may be fuzzy at best and where job security (an emotional shelter) is often the top priority of workers.

• *Disproportionately developed volitional dimension.* Here is an organization eager for change. Anything new is embraced with fervor and devotion. Tradition and old ways are seen as harmful and avoided at all costs. The organization's members have lots of enthusiasm, but much of it gets dissipated because energies are not focused. Many worthwhile projects are started, but few are finished.

One hospital I worked with exemplified this type. Every six months a new change and reorganization would take place, and after a few years I just accepted this as part of its culture. One of my former classmates was later hired as an administrator. When I asked him how his job was going, he replied, "Oh, quite stressful. We are going through a big and important reorganization." When I told him there was always a reorganization taking place, he seemed displeased at my comment. After all, if what I said were true, it would render his current work useless in six months.

• *Disproportionately developed spiritual dimension.* Such an environment is harder to find than some of the previously discussed situations. However, we could imagine an organization in which workers were very concerned with discovering universal truths, discussing these philosophies with one another, and making a meaningful contribution to the community. The economic goals of the company would be subordinated to social goals. These people would have wonderful intentions, but perhaps without the material resources, the intellectual capabilities, or the emotional stability to carry out their well-meaning and even laudable plans. Employees and managers, when faced with difficulties, might often say to one another, "Don't worry, God will take care of us. We must have faith." At the same time, they would not consider the second part of Muhammad's exhortation, "Trust in God, but tie your camel." Sometimes they might not even have a clear mission. No matter how competent or good-intentioned a group is, it needs a goal in order to be effective.

Organizational Change

We can look at the five dimensions of work for help in understanding how to make organizational change more effective. There are different though equally important concerns in each dimension. In the physical dimension, working conditions and extrinsic rewards are stressed; in the intellectual dimension, the emphasis is on learning and development; in the emotional dimension, support and appreciation are priorities; in the volitional dimension, the focus is on innovation and change; and in the spiritual dimension, the concern is for integrity, nobility, reciprocity, and love.

Exhibit 2.1 shows the five organizational dimensions and how each relates to organizational change ("higher" levels are on the bottom to correspond with the tree figure analogy). Much effort in change programs goes into such concepts as work design, extrinsic rewards, quality, innovation, and more challenging work, all of which are from dimensions one and two. Some programs deal with dimensions three and four issues of supportive and respectful relationships and need for change, but few address the spiritual dimension principles of integrity, trustworthiness, nobility, or justice.

Assessing the Balance

How do managers go about creating balance in their organizations? The first step is to observe the company and try to see clearly where it stands in regard to the five dimensions— to take the organization's temperature, so to speak.

Exhibit 2.2 lists some questions that managers can ask themselves to assess their organization. The unstarred questions assess positive elements of the organization and the starred questions assess negative elements. To score your answers to these questions,

Exhibit 2.1. Organizational Change in the Five Dimensions of Work.

Dimension	Organizational Change
1. Physical	Work design Working conditions Extrinsic rewards money, bonuses Financial well-being of company
2. Intellectual (Most organizational change takes place in the first two dimensions.)	Challenging work Training to see job differently Quality emphasis Innovation and creativity New responsibilities Opportunities to learn and develop Freedom-to-fail environment
3. Emotional (A small portion of change or training programs deal with this dimension.)	Supportive working relationships Mutually respectful relationship with boss Appreciation for work done
4. Volitional (Attention given here to resistance to change and sacrifice.)	Desire for change Willingness to make necessary sacrifices Top levels ready to change and make real sacrifices, too
5. Spiritual (Organizational change in this dimension is quite rare, yet it is necessary to bring long-term health to the company.)	Capacity and willingness to love Integrity, trustworthiness, and respect up and down the organization Justice at all levels Nobility and dignity of workers accepted Wisdom of love: love others as yourself

Exhibit 2.2. Questions for Examining the Five Dimensions of Work.

Material
 1. Does your company operate mostly in the black?
*2. Are you in continuous financial crisis?
 3. Do you have the resources to pay your employees decently? (Not do you *actually* pay them, merely *could* you.)
*4. Are compensation differentials between top and bottom excessively large? Increasing?
*5. Is there a high turnover rate for employees?
 6. Are the places of work (factories, offices) clean, comfortable, well kept, and adequately furnished?
 7. Is the equipment used modern, efficient, and safe?

Intellectual
 1. Do your engineers, technicians, or others keep up with cutting-edge technology?
 2. Do you spend adequate resources to send people for continuing education or to important professional conferences?
 3. Is spending on continuing education as a percentage of sales increasing?
 4. Are employees able to get reference materials, books, journals, and magazines that will help them learn more about their work and the environment?
 5. Do you reward employees who continue to learn?
 6. Are people happy to learn (rather than having to be coerced)?
 7. Do other organizations respect the knowledge of your employees?
 8. Do you respect the knowledge of your employees?
*9. Do employees often lack the necessary competence to complete projects adequately and on time?

Emotional
 1. Do there seem to be high levels of job satisfaction?
 2. Do people enjoy working with each other?
 3. Do employees like one another?
*4. Are there a disproportionate number of problems with depression, alcoholism, and frequent, even violent, outbursts?
*5. In meetings do people behave defensively or with power plays?
*6. Are people afraid to bring up in meetings what they really feel?
*7. Is there frequent concern about "not upsetting the boss"?

Volitional
 1. Is there a willingness to look at new ways of doing things?
 2. Do you rarely hear "It won't work" or "That's impossible to do"?

3. Is there a high level of energy on new projects?
*4. Do workers put energy into maintaining the status quo?
*5. Are new programs met with many complaints and much resistance?

Spiritual
1. Is there an acceptance and assumption of integrity among coworkers and bosses?
2. Do people trust one another? Do they trust management?
*3. Do employees feel exploited or treated unjustly?
4. Do customers expect and get a quality product?
*5. Is cynicism common among employees?
6. Do people joyfully help one another?
*7. Is there a lot of backbiting?
*8. Are there political fights? Political intrigues? Political posturing?
9. Is there an openness of communication that depends on a deep level of trust and commitment?
*10. Do people say different things to different people?
11. Is there a unity of "theory" and "practice" (i.e., do managers practice what they preach)?
12. Can groups discuss problems and handle conflict in a competent and dignified manner?
13. Is there a "spirit" of service to one another, to clients, to suppliers?

Note: * indicates negative scoring.

count how many positive elements were seen as adequately addressed, then count how many of the negative questions were answered with yes, and then determine what percentage of elements in each dimension are seen as positive and what percentage are seen as negative. You may find, for example, that materially your company does well 85 percent of the time, but emotionally it is only 40 percent effective. Please remember that this is not a scientific measurement but merely gives a general idea of how your organization is doing.

The questions in the exhibit relate to the symptoms of disequilibrium, such as regular financial crises, high turnover rates, an air of cynicism, backbiting, problems meeting deadlines, and so on. Indications that problems exist are almost always evident, if only we are willing to see them and accept the message being given to us. Similarly, in our personal lives we usually have evidence when our lives are out of balance. For me, imbalance shows up as forgotten appointments, being sharp with my children or colleagues, and daydreaming of long rest periods. For a manager, the symptoms that indicate personal lack of balance might be an increase in interpersonal conflicts at work and at home, working longer hours with less productivity, and habitually canceling personal appointments or time with family.

Moving Away from the "Or"

Because we are so accustomed to worrying about the material and intellectual growth of organizations, we have failed to realize the forces that could be unleashed if only we had in balance the emotional and spiritual dimensions of the organization.

We need to move to a higher level of thinking than is typified by the thought that we can have either love *or* discipline, warmth *or* productivity. Collins and Porras (1994) call this attitude the "Tyranny of the OR," which proclaims that we can have either creativity OR control, long-term OR short-term payoffs. They have found that highly visionary companies have the ability to operate in paradoxes, to follow the "Genius of the AND" and figure out how to have both sides of seeming contradictions: to create shareholder wealth AND do good for the world, to be pragmatic AND value-driven, to be visionary AND nuts-and-bolts oriented. They are not talking about a balanced midpoint between two opposites but rather about a synergistic integration of two important concepts.

As business consultant Jan Nickerson says, "My favorite word is *both*" (Liebig, 1994, p. 112). She says that when she works with groups, she tries to get them away from the teeter-totter view of balance to a view of the dimensions as sides of the infinity sign (Jan Nickerson, personal communication, January 1996). For example, you can have both profits *and* a spiritual workforce. What does a spiritual workforce produce, she asks? Whole people coming to work. And what do profits produce? An environment that allows the spirit to express itself. Looking from infinity rather than from the teeter-totter, there is no OR; there is only BOTH.

Tom and Kate Chappell (1993), founders and leaders of Tom's of Maine, Inc., operate on purely spiritual principles and are at the same time wildly successful. From 1985 to 1993 they experienced consistent annual growth in sales and profits of 25 percent; after a dip in 1994 they showed an impressive turnaround and sales increase in 1995. "The ultimate results of a business with soul is, I believe," states Tom, "a new kind of capitalism, a way of doing business that can analyze and strategize—but always with an eye on the common good. Once you taste this new way of doing business, once you find out how wonderful it is to manage for profit and the common good, you will want more. Goodness begets goodness" (Chappell, 1993, p. 214).

In coming chapters I examine how certain seemingly opposing conditions can exist together and actually create a healthier whole. A company can have unity AND independent thinking. There can be love AND productive work, as well as love AND management technologies. A company can be spiritual AND profitable.

> *The spirit and the body carry different loads*
> *and require different attentions.*
> *Too often we put saddlebags on Jesus and let the donkey*
> *run loose in the pasture.*
> *Don't make the body do what the spirit does best, and don't put*
> *a big load*
> *on the spirit that the body could carry easily.*
>
> —Rumi, 1988, pp. 70–71

Chapter Three

Love and the New Management Virtues

↫

Deeds of love and kindness and understanding
shall change the world.

—*Vinson Brown*

Virtue is its own reward.

—*Marcus Tullius Cicero, c. 50* B.C.

In the past few years a great deal of attention has been given to the
new management paradigm. We know the words well, but we don't
always know how to achieve what they represent: vision, empowerment, accountability, commitment, and customer orientation.
This chapter presents the perhaps radical notion that these goals
are achieved through love and spirituality.

Most of the moves from the old paradigm to the new involve
changing to a more spiritual foundation. For many managers and
management theorists, this is a new way of looking at things. Yet
once we open our minds to the perspective of spirituality, it becomes very clear: all the new management concepts that fall under
the umbrella of "new paradigm" are, at their core, outward manifestations of managers acting with the Wisdom of Love. They are a
package of behaviors, attitudes, decisions, and policies that reflect
the organization's spiritual essence. They are the workplace ver-
sions of spiritual virtues.

These virtues are discussed in ancient as well as modern writings, so they are not new concepts. But because they have not been

explored much in management thought or literature, I have termed them the New Management Virtues. They are as follows:

1. Trustworthiness
2. Unity
3. Respect and dignity
4. Justice
5. Service and humility

These management virtues form the philosophical and spiritual foundation for many of the new management concepts (Exhibit 3.1 shows how they correlate and possible behavioral outcomes). These virtues are not pie-in-the-sky ideals that are unworkable in the real world; they have proven to be effective in making organizations work better.

Trustworthiness

During my four years in the Czech Republic, I taught management training programs both in the Republic and in many other countries in the former Soviet bloc. Among other things, I taught business ethics. A common response during these sessions was, "Oh, you are just one of those naive Westerners. You don't understand our country, our culture. We do things differently here. And what's more, we *have* to cheat and lie now in order to catch up with the West. But in about five years after we reach their level of economic development, well, then we can be honest."[1]

During this same time period, however, after working with managers from many other regions, including Asia, I discovered an equally universal concept: trustworthiness. Every manager I have talked with from the various countries I have worked in has agreed that doing business is impossible without building up trust with suppliers, customers, and clients. Yang from China told me, "It will take you longer in the beginning, because we must see if we can

Exhibit 3.1. The New Management Virtues as Foundations for Management Practices.

New Management Virtue	Management Concepts	Behavioral Outcomes
Trustworthiness	Stewardship/Management accountability	Managers assume honesty Customers, employees expect integrity and no scandals or misuse of funds Toward ethical behavior
Unity	Creating shared vision Commitment Reciprocity	Unanimity in important decisions Customer satisfaction ROI as only one performance measure Manager controller to coach Consulting when management really listens, respect for authority
Respect and Dignity	Empowerment Consensus decisions Commitment leadership	Job enrichment Sociotechnical systems Group-centered problem solving Self-managed teams Manager as mentor, coach Utilization of discretionary effort
Justice	Profit-sharing Equal opportunity	Employee ownership, bonus Removal of barriers to equal opportunity
Service and Humility	Customer orientation Quality movement Sharing power; developing talented subordinates	Quality: customer's view, systematic approach to understanding, satisfying internal, external customers Continuous improvement Zero defect goal Service mentality: learning to be a servant

trust you. But once that is established, we will do business with you the rest of your life." Trustworthiness thus seems to be a thread running through business development throughout the world, even in countries not governed by "rule of law."

> Now we must rediscover the fact that we—all together—are human beings, and we must strive to concede to one another what moral capacity we have. Only in this way can we begin to believe that in other peoples as well as ourselves there will arise the need for a new spirit which can be the beginning of a feeling of mutual trustworthiness toward each other.

> —Albert Schweitzer, 1958

Trustworthiness becomes the foundation on which all of the other virtues are based. Without an expectation of truthfulness, without any trust, other virtues or good behaviors become meaningless. What good is a kind, considerate, and helpful associate who may cheat us tomorrow? Or a charming, charismatic business partner who lies? Or a good listener who then backbites us later? Also, because trustworthiness is the foundation of all the other virtues, it is the most vulnerable; once trust is broken, the other virtues are also lost.

Trustworthiness requires integrity and honesty, which can sometimes be acts of courage. Good leadership is based on honesty about both good and bad events or feedback, even when it hurts. Openness, even about the unpleasant, is important. If such openness happens, workers can withstand a lot. Jim Wilkerson, human resource director of ABB Vetco Gray, says, "I am always amazed at employees' ability to suffer if their leaders are open and are suffering, too" (personal communication, 1995).

Power and Control

A new kind of thinking is needed to bring about the kind of results we are talking about. Changes in worker participation and involvement will not take place, despite the flattening of organizational structures, as long as managers continue to think hierarchically (Osterberg in Liebig, 1994). Without such thinking, managers would no longer be controlling and giving orders but would instead be coordinating resources and processes, and ensuring that people get opportunities that test and develop their potential. Successful managers realize that their responsibility is not to control people but rather to control results (Watkins and Marsick, 1993).

The most recognizable use of power in organizations is political power, or the ability and willingness to influence others by punishing, firing, hiring, rewarding, withholding, or giving (Peck, 1993). Political power is not about character but about money and position. Both money and position are temporary and can be lost overnight, as has been seen not only in stock market crashes but also in company disasters where top executives get blamed and thrown out.

What we don't often hear about, however, is another kind of power—spiritual power—which comes from one's very being and is the capacity to influence others, not by controlling them as in political power, but through love, by example, as a result of kindness, consideration, humor, and wisdom—or the power of truth. Spiritual power knows no position. It is evident in both the poor and the wealthy, in people in both high and low positions. Those who have it do not feel arrogant and self-satisfied, but rather gain a greater humility, realizing that the true source of the power comes from a Higher Power, not from themselves.[2]

Political power comes from ambition, while spiritual power results from giving up ambition and surrendering oneself. The paradox here is that only by giving up ambition can one truly achieve any lasting power. However, once a manager has spiritual power, he or she would then use any given political power with greater wisdom and justice—and love.

Markets and Trust

The market system depends on trust—between customers and sellers, suppliers and manufacturers, bankers and companies. Without trust, the whole system would slow down. For example, if customers had no reason to believe that their purchases would be of decent quality and if they had no means of returning defective merchandise, imagine how wary they would be of spending money on anything. If suppliers were habitually paid late and sometimes less than the invoiced amount, they would demand cash on or before delivery, which would put many factories in a difficult cash flow situation. We take for granted a minimal level of trust and honesty in our daily business lives, forgetting how crucial they are to its functioning smoothly.

Trust has an economic value, as Fukuyama (1995) demonstrates, which we can see more easily if we think of its absence. Always negotiating contracts with the assumption that the other party will cheat and not live up to obligations and you arrive at $300 hammers and $800 toilet seats, as the Pentagon did not so long ago.

> *Truth alone obtains victory. . . . The path to the Divine is laid with truth.*
>
> —Hindu, *Mundaka Upanishad*, III, 1–6

> *Man, created by God in the best of moulds, can yet fall to the lowest depths, unless he lives a life of faith and righteousness.*
>
> —Islam, *Koran* XCV, 1–8

In contrast, Hugh Aaron (1994) describes his company that manufactured custom-made products after receiving telephone orders. The products were needed in one or two days and were worth up to several thousand dollars. The customer's word was good enough to start the order. In Aaron's twenty years as CEO, not once did a customer go back on an order. This was not unusual, he felt, for "without such trust, business couldn't be conducted" (p. 10).

Aaron also speaks of the importance of integrity in the ultimate prosperity of the company founded by his father and that he continued. "What finally allowed us to succeed was our character—we were honest, dependable, and conscientious workers—our knowledge of how the world works, and our mastery of a basic education" (p. 10).

Benneville Strohecker built Harbor Sweets from a tiny operation in his basement to a $2.6 million business today largely on trust. Instead of doing background checks on prospective employees, he hires by his gut. He has workers fill out their own time cards and allows for maximum flexibility in work schedules. "Trust," says Strohecker, "still remains the important ingredient in our recipes" (Strohecker, 1996, p. 9).

> *Trustworthiness is the greatest portal leading unto the tranquillity and security of the people. In truth the stability of every affair hath depended and doth depend on it.*
>
> —*Bahá'í, Bahá'u'lláh* (1978, p. 37)
>
> *Lord, who may dwell in your sanctuary? . . . He . . . who keeps his oath even when it hurts. . . . He . . . who does these things will never be shaken.*
>
> —Judaic/Christian, *The Bible*, Psalm 15:1, 2, 5

Looking forward to the year 2025, after the Second Industrial Revolution, Resource Consulting Network, a collaborative of five consulting firms, had seventy-five managers consider an environment where love, truth, and spirit were the norms. Resource Consulting Network asked them what were the key catalytic forces that started the revolution. Their responses say a lot about what they want and what is currently missing in our workplaces: "I said 'Trust me,' and they did." "I told my associates what I want *for* them not only *from* them." "I told my associates what it is that keeps me from telling them the whole truth."

James Autry (1991, p. 123) understands the dynamics of trust and truth when he says, "Trust beyond reason." Some people will abuse this, but only the ones who would find a way to take advantage another way.

Part of Hewlett-Packard (H-P) folklore is a story about locked inventory closets. One day the CEO ordered that all of the locks be taken off the closets. In some companies, managers might be horrified to do such a thing, expecting enormous larceny. But the H-P executive understood the wisdom and power of trust. Even if some things were stolen, he believed, it would only be minimal and the message given to the rest of the employees would be powerful enough to make the loss worthwhile. Today the closets remain unlocked and employees have lived up to the expectation of trustworthiness (George Starcher, personal communication, 1996).

Integrity is not typically expected in advertising. A 1995 Gallup poll placed advertising near the bottom of ethical professions, with only Congresspeople and used-car salesmen ranking lower. A new advertising agency in London is out to change that. St. Luke's offers a completely new model of what it believes the industry must become: "honest, ethical advertising that represents a company's Total Role in Society (TRS)" (Alburty, 1997, p. 118). This is partly manifested in the corporate mission statement: "Profit Is Like Health; You Need It, But It Is Not What You Live For." The founders' ideas of a company's TRS includes a company seeing itself as a force for social good, with the purpose to "benefit society," where profits are the requirement, but not the purpose, and where a company will have to be seen as a "trusted social citizen" before it will be able to sell or advertise productively (p. 122). These ideas cannot be dismissed as naive when they are expressed by the fastest-growing advertising agency in London, with first-year revenues at $72 million. Though geared toward the future, some of the company's inspiration can be traced back thousands of years to Aristotle and the Gospel of St. Luke.

There is no better ruler than Wisdom,
no safer Guardian than Justice,
no stronger sword than Righteousness,
no surer ally than Truth.

—Muhammad, founder of Islam[3]

Trust and Competence

Let us not forget that the other side of trust is competence. In order for a business to gain trust from customers and suppliers, it must have integrity, as well as be able to perform the job more than adequately. Real trust, then, is integrity times competence.[4]

Building Trustworthiness

It is not difficult to understand and accept the importance of trustworthiness in the workplace. Nor does it take great powers of piercing insight to see the need to treat employees with respect and dignity. But what does it mean, operationally, for your organization to build or block trustworthiness? Looking at the individual behaviors is more challenging than accepting the concept of trustworthiness. Frank and open meetings, for example, in which managers and subordinates share authentic feelings can go a long way toward enhancing trustworthiness, while withholding information does just the opposite. And anyway, organizational secrets have a way of not remaining secrets for long. Exhibit 3.2 lists some of the factors that can build or block trustworthiness in a company, and Exhibit 3.3 can be used to assess what factors influence trustworthiness in your company.

Unity

Top managers in 125 European companies were asked to identify their most important objectives, which were later matched with

Exhibit 3.2. Factors That May Influence Trustworthiness in Organizations.

	Builds Trust	Blocks Trust
Within My Control	1. We have weekly meetings in which my group is open and frank. 2. My subordinates share concerns, anger, etc. with me.	1. I haven't told my people the real news about next year's budget crunch. 2. Sometimes I store up negative feedback and give it out in too big bunches and with too much frustration.
Outside My Control	1. People are trusted to be honest on reimbursement requests, so there is little paperwork.	1. Top management withholds important information too long and rumors are rampant. 2. There is too much control from above and people do not feel free and trusted in many areas.

Exhibit 3.3. What Factors Influence Trustworthiness in My Company?

	Builds Trust	Blocks Trust
Within My Control		
Outside My Control		

the success of each company (Hardaker and Ward, 1991). The identification of critical success factors was found to be important to success, but equally important is a shared vision. As Hardaker and Ward explain, "The technique demands unanimity; all must agree to go in the same direction" (1987, p. 77). Shared vision was evident among the executives in the successful companies and absent in the poor performers.

The New Management Virtue of unity is the foundation for shared vision, group commitment, and universal participation. Without unity, none of these goals is possible. Without unity, the organization is pulled apart by centrifugal force or just plain entropy. That was happening to Chrysler before Lee Iacocca created a common vision and not only saved the company from bankruptcy but turned it back into a successful, innovative venture.[5]

Lack of unity has been at the root of the demise of IBM in recent years, as well as the previous decline of General Motors over a long period (though both, now under new chairmen, seem to have regained some of their former unity). Many executives are now seeing the importance of this unity, the power of which becomes evident once we see it in operation. For example, why has Wal-Mart been so successful? One reason is the unity of purpose and the common vision that founder Sam Walton has provided to all the locations and all the employees (Walton, 1992). IBM's change from a business machines company to a worldwide computer giant was largely due to the strong vision and sense of unity that Tom Watson provided when he ran the company from 1956 to 1971 (Watson, 1990).

Novell Inc. was once a threatening rival to Microsoft Corporation and was just as profitable. But after it bought up WordPerfect Corporation in 1994 in order to become an even bigger industry leader, the company imploded on itself because of lack of unity. Executives of WordPerfect came to see Novell's top managers as "rude invaders of the corporate equivalent of Camelot" (Clark, 1996, p. 4). Repeated clashes between the two groups resulted in the dismantling of WordPerfect's sales force, dooming its new products to the dust heap of marginal software. The fighting also distracted Novell from the business it should have been paying attention to, namely, supplying software for tying personal computers to networks. This left a vacuum that Microsoft was only too happy to fill.

The importance of unity is seen in other examples as well. "Reinventing the CEO," a study done in 1989 based on data from more than 1,500 CEOs and senior executives, showed that executives saw an overwhelming need for the "vital importance of visionary leadership" (Thompson, 1992, p. 213). Such leadership includes anticipating the organization's future goals and inspiring managers to reach them (Thompson, 1992), which are unifying functions of the manager. Creating and gaining acceptance for a unifying vision is one of the six main themes of the field of organizational transformation (Adams, 1984a). Another of the six themes is leadership, which involves stimulating alignment with the vision.

Motorola was saved by unity. In the mid-1980s it was on the verge of losing its cellular phone business to Japanese manufacturers, much as it had already surrendered its TV, stereo, and computer chip business to Japan. This time, however, Motorola decided to fight back, and it gained the commitment of its employees worldwide for a new quality program. Quality reports were shifted from last to first on officer meeting agendas, wallet-size cards listing program goals were printed in eleven languages, and 98,000 Motorolans celebrated quality day at twenty-three plants in 1989. The result? Top-quality products, or as a Fortune 100 director said, "Motorola is simply the best this country has to offer." Further, Motorola received the highest national business honor—winning the Baldrige National Quality Award in 1988 (Koestenbaum, 1991, pp. 162–163).

Unity as a prerequisite to other positive outcomes is an ancient concept. The Chinese I Ching says, "After considerable difficulties, the man collects his powers and overcomes the obstacles to the unity of all men. Sadness gives way to joy."

The Power of Unity

The power of unity is understood by anyone who has ever worked with a truly cohesive team that has a common vision (Senge, 1990). After such an experience, one has such a sense of energy and well-being that one's remaining career is spent seeking out that same kind of work environment. Creating that unity of vision requires a new kind of consciousness (Osterberg, 1993; Liebig, 1994), one based on love.

An environment of unity requires managers to change from being controllers to being coaches. The controlling, punitive approach is not conducive to heart-and-soul universal participation and building a common vision (Miller, 1991). Once a common vision is achieved, workers generally have a new sense of meaning in their work, and this sense is powerful indeed. As Jack London wrote, "God's own mad lover should die for the Kiss, but not for thirty-thousand a year" (London, 1984). God's own mad lover is someone in pursuit of a noble and worthy cause. When management is singularly focused on profits and money, it is difficult to gain high levels of motivation from workers. A sense of purpose resulting from shared vision and the virtue of unity is a vital factor in creating an energetic workforce.

Several years ago I spoke to a 3M executive from Germany who was working in St. Paul, Minnesota, at the company's headquarters. Without hesitation he said that one of the worst weaknesses of American business was its obsession with increasing shareholder wealth. He said, "It's hard to motivate workers to get up every morning, jump out of bed and say, 'I can't wait to get to work to help increase shareholder wealth.'"

A testament of unity was given by Tom Peters (1987), who said that any company that wants to be excellent must have the full involvement and support of everyone in the organization. Managers must be careful, however, to avoid the pseudo-unity that is all too present in organizations, where slogans, mission statements, parties, pats on the back, and first-name familiarity are mistaken for an organic harmony. In this condition, conflicts are smoothed over and suppressed, and organizational traumas go unacknowledged.

Some time ago, Covenant Corporation fired 600 people. Shortly after that the CEO spent $1 million dollars on a "Family Day," with the purpose of creating unity (Jackall, 1988). The gala event featured clowns, sports celebrities, and games, and was attended by 14,000 employees. Afterward, the CEO sent a memo congratulating himself, stating that Family Day had helped the "family" at Covenant to develop, and that it had showed how great goals could be achieved if everyone worked together as a team. Such hypocrisy is not lost on the majority of employees.

Contrast this with Nucor Corporation during the U.S. recession of 1993 to 1994. In order to deal with greatly decreased revenues, the company placed all its employees (from the CEO to maintenance workers) on two- or three-day weeks. No workers were laid off. When Nucor rebounded, it enjoyed an unusual esprit de corps (Fukuyama, 1995).

Reciprocity

True unity requires reciprocity, which means treating others as they want to be treated and considering the consequences of behavior, the concepts upon which the Wisdom of Love is based. Susan Herman (1994) thinks that reciprocity is the key to an organization's spirituality. She sees organizational spirit as the same as school spirit or camp spirit:

> It's an issue of reciprocity, at its bottom line. It's the feeling that I am respected, appreciated, supported and nurtured in this place, that my growth and learning are considered to be important; and it results in my feeling that this organization is a wonderful one and that I am happy to put as much of my attention and energy into helping the organization grow and develop as is necessary at any given point in time. It's the feeling that people think and speak

well of me here, and that I think and speak well of the organization both inside it and particularly outside it. It's a feeling of "we're all in this together, pulling for basically the same organizational goals, which we believe in and consider to be valuable." In organizational spirit, WE are the force. It's our synergy that creates a high-spirited organization.

Without reciprocity, the synergy that is so important in real unity is absent. Love makes reciprocity that much easier. When you care about someone, there is more natural desire to do for them, to keep the giving going back and forth.

Building Unity

Unity can be built in various ways, such as through a shared vision, reliance on consensus decisions, discouraging backbiting, and encouraging social events; ego, pushing one's own ideas, poor listening skills, and political maneuvering can destroy unity. Exhibit 3.4 lists some of the factors that can build or block unity in a company, and Exhibit 3.5 can be used to assess what factors influence unity in your company.

Respect and Dignity

Pay homage to God . . . and subordinates.

—Islam, Al-Quran 4:36 (1988)

Mary Kay Ash, known for giving respect and recognition to her sales force, built her company from sales of about $200,000 in 1963 to $613 million in 1993 (Farnham, 1993). Mary Kay emphatically stresses the need for the Golden Rule and puts God first in her life.

J. C. Bradford, who founded the investment company that bears his name, understood the importance of respect in his fledgling business back in the 1930s. After the stock market crashed in 1929 and then bottomed out in 1933, business picked up somewhat

Exhibit 3.4. Factors That May Influence Unity in Organizations.

	Builds Unity	*Blocks Unity*
Within My Control	1. My unit has a reasonably good shared vision.	1. Sometimes I am impatient and don't search out all views in meetings.
	2. We try to use consensus for most decisions in my unit.	2. When I am too attached to an idea, I have a hard time listening to others.
	3. There is a minimum of subgrouping in my unit.	
	4. I discourage backbiting.	
Outside My Control	1. Strong company spirit exists.	1. There are too many cliques in our organization.
	2. Frequent social events are planned and attended.	2. Too much political maneuvering takes place.

Exhibit 3.5. What Factors Influence Unity in My Company?

	Builds Unity	*Blocks Unity*
Within My Control		
Outside My Control		

and Bradford's company was surviving, though marginally. After the second crash, in 1937, however, the situation was bleak and the future seemed hopeless for some years. With his business dried up, Bradford did not take the usual course of action and lay off or fire his stock salesmen. He called them together and put them on a salary. "Go out and call on people," he told the sales staff. Just talk to them, he said, and let them know who we are. Back then, this was nearly a unique practice. The sales staff did this, on their weekly salaries, until the economy picked up as the United States entered World War II. When people did buy stocks again, they remembered J. C. Bradford and his salespeople. Today the company is growing so fast it can hardly keep up with itself, and its mission is to be the best in service to clients (J. C. Bradford, personal communication, 1996).

The success of Wal-Mart, according to Sam Walton (1992, p. 103), is due to its attitude of respect and dignity toward its employees: "If you want the people in the stores to take care of the customers, you have to be sure you're taking care of the people in the stores. That is the most important single ingredient of Wal-Mart's success."

CEO Howard Schultz attributes the recent prosperity of Starbucks Coffee Company to, in part, respecting workers and fostering strong employee relations (Scott, 1995, p. 28): "I . . . [made] sure everyone felt valued, respected and part of the winning result." Starbucks has grown at an annual compounded rate of 60 percent for the past five years.

Czech managers have told me that one of the worst things about working under a communist regime was the complete disregard for human beings. Employees were treated with disdain and customers were shown contempt. No wonder there was a black cloud of depression in many countries under communistic rule. How could anyone expect a strong work ethic under these conditions? This may seem an extreme example, but all too often in American companies employees are treated as children to be controlled and punished, from whom information is withheld and from whom managers extract the last ounces of energy. If we want to have companies that can compete with strength in the global marketplace, these dynamics cannot continue.

A company that does not respect its employees will suffer lower levels of motivation, alienation of workers, and sometimes a sense of depression in the workplace. Too often I have heard employees say something like, "If he thinks I will do anything extra, he's crazy!" This is stated after repeated incidents of being treated with no dignity. But looking at companies like Federal Express, where employees are respected and expected to make important decisions and take risks, we see delivery persons—on their own and knowing they are making the right decision—renting helicopters to make sure that deliveries get to their destinations on time. Ricardo Semler's Brazilian manufacturing company, Semco, which has demonstrated breathtakingly innovative structures and policies (see Chapter Four for more details), has shown such extraordinary success partly because, in Semler's words, "We hire adults and then we treat them like adults" (1989, p. 79).

Teamwork is espoused by many organizations. Some even do it. However, real worker participation may be as rare as cappuccino cafes at the top of the Himalayas. Advanced forms of employee involvement programs are uncommon because they are "inconsistent with the dominant management ideology and the fundamental design principles of most contemporary organizations" (Galbraith, Lawler, and Associates, 1993, p. 150).

Sometimes managers pay lip service to worker participation through pseudo–participation programs designed to fit their own management paradigm of control. In a recent survey, nearly 90 percent of companies claimed to use empowerment, but 30 percent said there is almost no employee involvement in decision making ("Managers," 1995). Chris Argyris and Donald Schön (1974) have shown that it is easy for managers to have a wide discrepancy between their intentions and their actions, and that it is common for them not to see that disparity. Managers talk about involving employees but actually leave few decisions to them and may never realize their own level of self-delusion. As expected, workers quickly see through the facade and are able to distinguish between rhetoric and real behavior. The managers who do try empowerment may do so only half-heartedly and then, not surprisingly, fail.[6]

One of my friends worked as a supervisor in a factory where managers bullied workers regularly and reneged on promises almost daily. He told me that two months previously the managers had gone to a seminar, come back all fired up, and hung up signs around the plant that said, "We are a team that works *together*" and "Our mission is to . . . and each employee is important to achieving that goal." My friend said that the supervisors and workers just laughed at the signs and paid as little attention as possible to the managers.

Environmentalist Roger Telschow implemented empowerment almost out of desperation, in a last-ditch attempt to save his small printing company (Telschow, 1993). After he hired his first three employees, all of whom were told to call him "Mr. Telschow" (p. 6), he found that alternating ultimatums and niceness didn't produce much from them, so he basically did it himself. Spending long hours doing the work to ensure quality service wore on him after a while, and he decided to sell the growing company. But, like many entrepreneurs, he was tough. Rather, he went to the employees and told them it was their responsibility to manage their own jobs; he would help them when necessary, adding "and just call me Roger" (p. 6). What began was training, discussions on customer requirements, profiting-sharing bonuses, and a "frustration log" to list difficulties in job completion ("Blueprints for Success," 1995, p. 32). A particularly effective technique was Telschow's announcement that he would pay $5 on the spot to anyone who found a mistake in a work order. Telschow figures each $5 spent saved $100 in wastage. Instead of selling Ecoprint, Telschow implemented empowerment and now has a ten-employee company that has won at least four national and state productivity awards since 1991. As Telschow says, "Our principle competitive edge is our people" (Greig, 1996, p. 42).

> *If we live in the Spirit, let us also walk in the Spirit.*

—Christian, *The Bible*, Galatians 5:25

> *Let us not love in word, neither in tongue; but in deed and in truth.*

—Christian, *The Bible*, 1 John 3:18

> *Beware . . . lest ye walk in the ways of them whose words differ from their deeds . . . for the professions of most men, be they high or low, differ from their conduct.*

—Bahá'í, *Bahá'u'lláh*, 1976, p. 305

New Ways of Working

Despite the difficulties of breaking down the old command management paradigm, we can see continuing evidence that it is in fact happening. Companies are realizing that it makes good business sense to treat people with respect. Besides being praiseworthy in itself, honoring worker dignity can pay off with a financially healthier company.

The old, dehumanizing assembly line, which many saw as a bedrock of modern manufacturing organizations, is giving way to the "spiral line" (Williams, 1994, pp. 1, 8). As Sony and NEC are using it now, four workers share a small "shop" while each of them assembles an entire video camera or cordless phone. Contrary to dire predictions that such work would be risky for productivity, these companies are finding positive gains. Sony's spiral line has a 10 percent higher productivity rate than their conventional assembly line. This is because workers move at their own pace, thus reducing errors, and when there is a problem the whole line is not shut down. Similar "craft-based" layouts are used by Compaq Computer Corporation, which boasts a 51 percent labor productivity increase as a result. As one consultant put it, there is "no future in conventional conveyor lines. They are a tool which conforms to the person with the least ability." These are examples of how treating people with respect is also good for the company. As one NEC worker remarked of the new craft system, "This way is better. You have your own job, work at your pace, fix your own mistakes."

The one-size-fits-all workplace often just doesn't work well—not only its assembly lines, but also its work hours. Respect in the form of flexible work hours pays off. Sought after by some employees and too often shunned by management, part-time work can be an effective way to relieve labor costs and various financial pressures. In a study by McKinsey & Company in Germany, productivity increased from 3 percent to 20 percent as a result of preventing employee burnout, managing demand peaks and valleys better, and increasing operating hours. Increases were shown in both team energy and worker motivation, as evidenced by absenteeism reductions of up to 50 percent (Hagemann, 1994).

Mary Pischke wanted to start a company that had a heart and a soul and use it to create harmonious relationships with customers and employee (Simmons, 1996; Sunoo, 1994). Her American branch of the German Birkenstock has grown slowly since the 1960s, and she has always been careful to hire people who were more of the nonprofit type who could still work in a for-profit. One of her biggest problems now is hiring people for the $100 million company and making sure that they share in her holistic business vision.

> *To enjoy the benefits of providence is wisdom; to enable others to enjoy them is virtue.*
>
> —Zoroastrian, The Zend-Avesta (in Müller, 1981)

> *If you love those who love you, what credit is that to you? . . . Be merciful, even as your Father is merciful.*
>
> —Christian, *The Bible*, Luke 6:32, 36

Nobody should seek his own good, but the good of others.

—Christian, *The Bible*, 1 Corinthians
10:24

Building Respect

Treating people with respect is arguably the one virtue most abused in organizations yet the one perhaps easiest to remedy. Empowering employees and then rewarding and appreciating their efforts shows respect, while being insensitive and too demanding, with no recognition for contributions, wreaks havoc on respect. Exhibit 3.6 lists some of the factors that can build or block respect and dignity in a company, and Exhibit 3.7 can be used to assess what factors influence respect and dignity in your company.

Justice

All of us have within us some sort of justice monitor.[7] This monitor develops early in life; parents often hear their children say, "That's not fair!" Adults are not much different; we just don't show our sense of justice as often. Either we have learned better coping skills for dealing with injustice or we mask our feelings better. Representative Millicent Fenwick stated, "I have come to believe that the one thing people cannot bear is a sense of injustice. Poverty, cold, even hunger, are more bearable than injustice" (1980).

Justice cannot stand alone, without any other virtue. To treat others with justice requires empathy, that is, love. Justice is impossible without empathy, for true justice cannot be meted without being able to put oneself in the other person's place (Gesine Schwan, personal communication, April 1995). Otherwise, how can I really know what is fair for the other person in any situation? The kind of fairness implied in the Golden Rule actually creates the basis for justice, because when I act toward another in a manner I would want, disparities of opportunity or treatment are minimized. A sense of common dignity as humans is manifested in this empathy

Exhibit 3.6. Factors That May Influence Respect and Dignity in Organizations.

	Builds Respect and Dignity	*Blocks Respect and Dignity*
Within My Control	1. I allow my people to make their own decisions and to have the freedom to fail.	1. I have been accused of being insensitive at times and not noticing what demotivates my employees.
	2. I try to show my appreciation for work well done.	2. When I am pushed against a deadline, I push others too hard, too.
Outside My Control	1. The company has a good incentive program.	1. Sometimes top management gets stuck in its own ideas and forgets the impact on the rest of the company.
	2. People are expected to succeed and are treated with a positive sense of optimism.	2. People in a few departments complain that their ideas are stolen by management and that they are not given due credit.

Exhibit 3.7. What Factors Influence Respect and Dignity in My Company?

	Builds Respect and Dignity	*Blocks Respect and Dignity*
Within My Control		
Outside My Control		

and justice, for if I feel myself as superior and the other as a mere "resource," I am ignoring her dignity.

Justice can also create trust (Gesine Schwan, personal communication, April 1995). When we treat others fairly, they will come to expect justice from us and to trust us. If justice is combined with open methods of decision making, we greatly reduce the chances of demagogue leadership. Schwan's method for determining whether our behaviors or policies are just is to apply the "newspaper test." Would we want our actions published for all to read (personal communication, April 1995)?

Compensation Systems

Treating employees fairly can include equitable compensation, profit-sharing, and affirmative action for minorities or disadvantaged groups. What happens when employees sense injustice in their pay system? Often resentments build up and motivation declines.

In Semco's Brazilian plants, management regularly sends employees salary survey reports of comparable jobs in Brazil. Workers are then asked how much they feel they deserve and are given the requested amount, even if it is too much. If the person hasn't earned the extra worth by the next year, they have a serious session with a manager. There is scant chance for workers to feel personal injustice in Semco's factories, which are among the most successful in Brazil (Semler, 1993, 1994).

> *O ye believers*
> *Stand out firmly for justice*
>
> —Islam, *Koran* IV, 135

> *The best beloved of all things in My sight is Justice; turn not away therefrom.*
>
> —Bahá'í, *Bahá'u'lláh*, 1990, pp. 3–4

Paying for performance has been shown to reap positive benefits for the company through the use of bonuses, merit awards, employee ownership, and profit-sharing plans. We don't need complicated statistical analysis to understand that employees will work harder if they expect to receive a piece of the profits, if there is a consequence to their level of output. Justice may be the principle that profit sharing is based on and what makes it work, but it is the cost-reduction potential of profit sharing that attracts executives (Kanter, 1987), since workers are more cognizant of saving costs when it has a consequence to their paycheck.[8]

Employee ownership as a means of paying for performance has been embraced by a number of large and functioning companies, including McDonnell Douglas, TWA, Avis, Morgan Stanley, and Arthur D. Little, which have become at least one-third (33 percent) employee owned (Richter, 1994). Some professional firms of lawyers, consultants, and investment bankers have gone public because of problems with personal liability of partners and succession of ownership. Those that have solved these problems—such as McKinsey & Company, where all ownership is in the hands of active partners—seem to have come out on top. McKinsey, with more than $1 billion in earnings, remains one of the preeminent top management consulting firms in the world (George Starcher, personal communication, December 1995).

CEO Pay

The recent U.S. trend to pay CEO's millions of dollars even when the company's profit's are decaying is considered by many to be unjust. In fact, the U.S. congress passed a bill to make payments over $1 million not tax-deductible, though it has not seriously deterred these huge payments. The problem here is one of CEO's and boards not following the principles of justice. What are the results?

One result is that such payments are a drain on the stockholders. If a company is in difficult straits and gives away excessive amounts to executives, this means there is less dividend for stockholders, less money to invest in new ventures and updating plants, and, very important, less money to pay decent salaries to workers. There were many cases of executives getting tens or hundreds of millions of dollars in bonuses while workers were asked to either forgo raises or get less-than-adequate ones. Some argue that in a huge corporation the percentage of total revenue that goes to the CEO's salary is so low it does not affect the total financial picture significantly, but even so, it is the symbolic nature of what the huge salary represents relative to worker belt-tightening that is unjust.

Some years ago a reporter asked the president of one of the large Japanese automakers why he was earning only the equivalent of less than $100,000 per year when the CEOs of U.S. automakers were earning multiple millions. The president said that his company's success depended on the motivation and commitment of all its workers and it would be hard to gain that commitment if he was earning so much more than they were.

Workforce Reduction

During the U.S. recession of 1992, countless jobs were cut. It was difficult, but somehow people understood the necessity of saving companies through drastic cost-cutting measures. There was an awareness that U.S. businesses had to radically change and become lean in order to compete in the ferocious global marketplace. Along with this attitude was the assumption that when times got better the layoffs would stop. If justice were at work, that would be true. Instead, what we see more recently is record profits and near-record layoffs by some companies (Murray, 1995). Mobil, for example, posted soaring earnings and soon after announced cuts of 4,700 workers. Surely this is not just.

Late in 1995 AT&T announced a layoff of 40,000 employees out of 300,000 because of the corporation's imminent split-up into three separate companies. Chairman Bob Allen evidently felt no shame about it, saying that he was really saving the company for the remaining employees. At the same time, he made a profit of $5 million on his stocks as a result of the announcement. The company's problems are partly a result of his disastrous $7.5 billion purchase of NCR, which drained the company of billions of dollars. Yet his salary in 1994 was $5.3 million. Asked if he thought he should apologize to the 30,000 workers who were losing their jobs, he commented that he thought there was no point in doing so (Sloan, 1996).

Contrast the above injustice with a situation in Brazil at Semco. When the economy in Brazil collapsed in 1990, Semco, like all other companies, was in dire straits. Owner Ricardo Semler (1994) offered employees the option of layoffs or all workers taking a 13 percent cut in pay while managers took a 40 percent cut (Semler included). Other strategies for survival included outsourcing to former employees, who were allowed to use company buildings and equipment to do their work. As a result, nearly everyone retained some kind of job, and once again the company is thriving.

Semler would doubtless agree with ServiceMaster Chairman C. William Pollard (1994, p. 5), who is responsible for the 200,000 employees of an enormously successful and fast-growing company: "It is wrong for me to be involved in actions or decisions where one person secures a benefit or an advantage at the expense of another, and it is fundamentally right for me to be involved in serving and helping others."

What happens to workers' motivations after they are treated unjustly with massive layoffs in the face of huge salaries for executives? Many employees feel varying levels of hopelessness or lack of appreciation, and the level and quality of their work suffers. Under these conditions, managers can't even consider an energized workforce. "With good morale, everything is possible, with poor morale, nothing is" (Koestenbaum, 1991, p. 15).

Loyalty is one of the first casualties in these situations (Murray, 1995). Employees felt betrayed, became nervous and worried, and drastically decreased their productivity because they constantly discussed the situation. As one Mobil shop steward said, "People have been talking more than 50 percent of the time. It's water-cooler talk all day long" (Murray, 1995, p. 5).

At least one company has a strong and explicit set of values that has been translated into virtues and does not allow this type of corporate bloodletting. Respect, trust, integrity, and justice are expected from everyone on the staff at Idea Connection Systems. But it is not a one-way transaction, for the same respect and justice are given to the employees. President Robert Rosenfeld (personal communications, 1995, 1996) and vice president Michael Winger-Bearskin (personal communication, 1995; Rosenfeld and Winger-Bearskin, January 1995) firmly believe that reducing the number of employees in order to achieve profit is unacceptable. If it's a matter of reducing the workforce to survive, that's different. Rosenfeld told me that he considers the company to be like a body. "If it has gangrene on the arm, you have to cut off the arm for the rest of the body to live. But to cut off the arm in a healthy body because you think the increased blood flow helps the whole body is just plain wrong" (personal communication, January 1995).

Economically speaking, it is expensive to lay off managers or technical people, with the average cost around $30,000 to $100,000 (Downs, 1995, p. 58), and to rehire them (which can cost as much as $50,000). Since most laid-off positions are filled again within two years, the result is a binge and purge syndrome. Companies that use layoffs "mercilessly bleed critical personnel. [They stagger] from the loss of talent, knowledge and morale for months, even years." Layoffs start a vortex that sucks "the fat, then the muscle, then the brainpower from the organization" (Downs, 1995, p. 58). Since 1985, when Kodak started the first of its 12,000 layoffs at a cost of $2.1 billion, it has reduced profits by 50 percent while revenues have remained constant.

U.S. and European companies that restructured without downsizing tended to show higher profit margins and greater return on assets than those that downsized (Mumford and Hendricks, 1996). Saved costs for downsizers often went to expensive consultants and outsourced tasks, while those companies that were concerned with their employees and acted out of justice and respect tended to cap-italize on their increased worker loyalty.

Poor Performers

In a virtuous organization based on love, what should be done with managers or employees who do not perform adequately? Even the love-and-caring gurus such as James Autry and Ricardo Semler know that sometimes you have to let people go. It is a matter of justice to the other workers and to the company. Any virtue out of balance with the others is no longer healthy, just as eating only meat but no fruits or vegetables would not be the best for the body. Allowing an inadequate employee to remain on the payroll may be love without proportionate justice. There are ways to achieve this balance with respect and dignity, however. Japanese businesses, which are run on the team or group model, regularly evaluate executive performance. When managers are found wanting, they are quietly moved else-where where they can cause few problems (Drucker, 1993).

Loyalty is not only a nice idea; it affects a company's financial health. Reichheld's research (1996) shows that the most successful employers inspire loyalty among employees, customers, and in-vestors. As for employees, when there is lower turnover, the profits go up. For the companies in his study, improving employee re-tention by only 5 percent increased profit margins by 50 percent. Lower employee turnover generally results in higher customer retention, as well. State Farm Insurance, for example, has agents who stay on average nineteen years, much longer than their com-petition. Reichheld believes this is a major reason why State Farm's profits are 40 percent higher than other insurance companies.

Believing the company cares about them as people is one of the prime reasons Hallmark Cards, Inc., inspires such high loyalty in its workers (Flynn, 1996). Listed as one of the best places to work for ten straight years by *Working Mother* magazine, Hallmark has thou-sands of twenty-five-year employees who belong to the Quarter Century Club. How does the company exhibit this sense of caring to its employees? It listens. Every three months there are Corporate Town Hall meetings where twelve hundred workers gather in three separate groups to hear and give feedback to CEO Irvine Hockaday and other top management. Small groups of employees meet ten times a year for ninety-minute face-to-face meetings with Hockaday. In total, nearly six thousand employees each year have the change to dialogue with the CEO on various issues.

Hallmark's caring is shown materially, as well, through generous benefits packages, including educational benefits, profit sharing, take-home meals from the company cafeteria, backup elder and child care, and birthday or work-achievement celebrations with lots of affection (Flynn, 1996). Finally, the caring shows up in Hallmark's no-layoff history. Even though the company, or various locations, may have slow times, more creative and humane options than layoffs are used. Employees have the choice to take time off with no pay, while maintaining benefits. Workers can retrain and move to a department with more need, often retaining the higher old salary. Some individuals have chosen to volunteer for community activities, while receiving their regular Hallmark pay. Though these approaches cost money, the company believes the goodwill and security employees feel makes the cost more than worthwhile. Director of employee relations Dave Pylipov says that Hallmark tries to enhance the "relationship between the company and employees" and to make it "as mutually productive as possible. Then everybody wins" (Flynn, 1996, p. 61).

Diversity

The principle of justice is seen in operation in the increased emphasis in recent decades on minority rights in the workplace. After EEOC and affirmative action laws were instituted in the United States in the 1960s and 1970s, some companies began to see that promoting minorities had a positive influence on performance. Numerous academic studies have shown that heterogeneous groups outperform homogeneous groups in problem solving and creative solutions (Wheeler, 1996). The link between diversity and creativity is not lost on Merck Company, whose "lifeblood is innovation and creativity." As CEO Raymond Gilmartin says, " We need access to talent from everywhere. We want to make sure it is not restricted" (Wheeler, 1996, p. 102).

Compelling business realities for moving companies toward more diversity include the global economy, a more diverse customer base, productivity needs, and workforce composition changes (Wheeler, 1995, 1996). Such companies as Allstate, R. R. Donnelly & Sons, and St. Paul Companies include diversity as a vital component for a "balanced scorecard" of success (Wheeler, 1996, p. 127). Global effectiveness of work teams was studied by Intel Corporation, which found that its high-performing teams had common characteristics of diversity, trust, respect, cooperation, goals, and focus (Wheeler, 1996).

Quality guru W. E. Deming (Tulin, 1994, p. 9) summed up the situation by saying, "Any organization that excludes or underutilizes its human talent because of race, gender or national origin, simply undermines its ability to optimize the system."

Building Justice

Since all of us have an internal justice meter that lets us know when we are not getting our due, it is therefore important for managers to have that sense of justice toward others in the organization. When budgets are cut, if upper levels sacrifice it is easier for the lower levels to do so as well and to feel that justice is being served. Other behaviors that create a sense of justice are listening to all sides in disputes and encouraging and rewarding those from within the organization with higher positions rather than hiring mostly from the outside. Exhibit 3.8 lists some of the factors that can build or block justice in a company, and Exhibit 3.9 can be used to assess what factors influence justice in your company.

Exhibit 3.8. Factors That May Influence Justice in Organizations.

	Builds Justice	*Blocks Justice*
Within My Control	1. When there were some cutbacks, we discussed options as a group and came to a decision. 2. If there is a conflict, I try to listen to both sides before making any decisions.	1. I have been known to spend more on myself than others get for nice furniture and travel. 2. Last year I discontinued some privileges of a few people, who called it unfair.
Outside My Control	1. Insiders are given preference for openings. 2. Most people feel they have a voice to air grievances.	1. Outsiders get higher salaries if they are brought in for a position. 2. We had cutbacks recently when our top management got hefty bonuses.

Exhibit 3.9. What Factors Influence Justice in My Company?

	Builds Justice	*Blocks Justice*
Within My Control		
Outside My Control		

Service and Humility

As a result of new management approaches, businesses have moved from focusing on discrete tasks to focusing on process and customer needs (Miller, 1991). Outstanding, competitive firms focus their attention on serving the real needs of their customers. They have customer-friendly systems and employees who are attentive, responsive, and willing to help, both of which signal the increased importance of the New Management Virtue of service.

The orientation to satisfy the customer has become almost an evangelistic mission for Tom Peters, whose book *Liberation Management* (1992) declares that the customer is the employer. He asks us to imagine our paychecks as given by the customer and then to see what a difference that makes in our attitude and behavior toward the customer.[9]

As this orientation to customers has increased, so have customers' expectations of quality service. These expectations push organizations to newer heights of service orientation. A cycle of increasing expectations and quality develops.

> *For the sake of the welfare of all, carry on thy task in life.*
>
> —Hindu, *Bhagavad Gita*, 3:20, 1984,
> p. 58

> *Again, is there any deed in the world that would be nobler than service to the common good? This is worship: to serve mankind.*
>
> —Bahá'í, 'Abdu'l-Bahá, 1969, p. 177

If we can see work within this frame of service, it becomes a positive force for all concerned. When work is performed in the spirit of true service, not only does it benefit society, but it also helps the employer and the customer, and can give a new sense of meaning to employees.

As Viktor Frankl (1984) reminds us, it is the *meaning* in life that is important, because having a higher purpose keeps us psychologically healthy. I believe it gives us spiritual health as well. Work without meaning, without significance, is worse than boring. It is *demeaning*. Taking care of others and seeing it as an important service can create a sense of meaning in work, giving employees a reason to exert themselves. Developing this spirit of service can be an important factor in creating a higher purpose for workers.

That higher purpose can be the superordinate goal that unites fighting factions. GE Plastics division bought out an old competitor, Borg-Warner Chemicals, and employees on both sides developed negative feelings about the forthcoming joining of the two. Morale plummeted, while cynicism increased. Manager Joel Hurt saved the day with what became known as the Share to Gain program (Bollier, 1996).

Four hundred and seventy employees from both divisions got together and planned the renovation of a dilapidated YMCA in a rough neighborhood of Southern California. In one twelve-hour workday, the entire group painted, removed old lockers, built walls, laid tile, repaired the irrigation system, rebuilt the basketball court, and put in new ceilings. The results was a YMCA unrecognizable from what it had been just twenty-four hours before. But the benefit to the GE group was a new sense of camaraderie. While old rivalries melted away, the team was drawn together by building something of lasting value.

> *Work draws us nearer to God, and enables us to better grasp His purpose for us in this world.*
>
> —Shoghi Effendi Rabbani (in Badii, 1993)

ServiceMaster, a $4 billion a year company that deals in health care management, custodial services, pest control, and lawn care, goes one step further in developing the sense of service in its employees. Each person, from the chairman on down, must spend at least one day a year performing one of the company's services, whether it is cleaning a hospital, getting rid of roaches, or fertilizing a lawn (Dubashi, 1994). This is just one way the company reminds employees that each of them is important and that doing their job well helps the company. I think it also goes a long way in reminding executives what their business is about—serving others.

The vice president (VP) of human resources at a Fortune 100 company told me a few years ago that he was responsible for planning a strategy session for all the other VPs, who would fly in from around the world. Their task? To make their company more service oriented. He shook his head in despair as he asked me, "How are these men [and they were all men] going to create a company based on service when they don't know how to do it themselves? They have wives at home who do everything for them. Basically they just show up and pay the bills. At the office, their secretaries function as office wives, running errands, buying gifts, even making their investments for them. How can I possibly help them to understand what service is all about?"

This VP needed to send the other VPs to the executive charm school that management consultant Robert Rosenfeld has talked about starting (personal communication, March 1994). Rosenfeld's idea was to have a restaurant as part of the school, and the executives would work as waiters and waitresses so they could learn how to serve.

Organizations that develop the New Management Virtue of service and give extraordinary satisfaction are the ones that will succeed. PepsiCo International has been moving into the former Soviet bloc countries and, according to Arvid Yaganegeh, formerly one of its regional franchisers for Pizza Hut and KFC, has been "cleaning up the competition because of our quality and our service" (personal communication, 1994). PepsiCo estimates that 65 percent of their repeat business is due to quality and reliability in service.

Serving customer needs helped Rebecca Mathias's Mothers Work Inc. go from an almost failed mail-order business to a 450-shop retail chain (Bird, 1996; Mangelsdorf, 1992). In the beginning, Mathias advertised in major publications and got one hundred catalogue requests, but no sales. Instead of giving up, she went right to the customer to see what was wrong. She personally called all one hundred people and asked them why they didn't buy anything. That lesson on attentiveness to customer needs still stays with the company today.

The British manufacturer Cookson Group, which has 13,000 employees in two hundred factories worldwide, almost went bankrupt in 1990 (Cookson Group, 1996; Whitley, 1994). After a new CEO, Richard Oster, was named, major changes helped save the company. One of these changes was a new devotion to customer service. The company's goal is to be "extraordinarily sensitive" to customer needs and to do whatever they can to fill them, as well as to anticipate what future needs will be. After six years, Oster's philosophy has shown its power in the marketplace of service. Cookson has increased it sales, earnings, and dividends. Its profits have soared 60 percent in the six years since the transformation to a service orientation.

Service is not only for outside the organization. With the New Management Virtues, supervisors become servants to the employees, which requires a shift in thinking about what management is. The job of managers, says Peter Drucker (1989), is to remove blocks and help the employees get their work done more easily. Managers should be enhancing the strengths of employees while making the employees' weaknesses irrelevant—not to criticize nor overlook, but to make the deficiencies *irrelevant*. For example, Robert Rosenfeld manages his Idea Connection Systems, Inc., with Drucker's concept. If someone is highly creative but useless with details, Bob does not disparage the lack but celebrates the positive. In this case, he makes sure to assign work that calls for high creativity and is not concerned with details, leaving that to others who do it well.

PepsiCo also shows how service can extend beyond customers to employees. Its corporate headquarters in Purchase, New York, hired a concierge to serve all of its eight hundred employees, from CEO to mail clerk. The concierge performs any tasks from buying concert tickets to hiring nannies to arranging to have a roof fixed. This ultimate employee benefit was embraced in early 1993 after a survey showed that workers were too stressed and had little time for personal errands. PepsiCo knows, as do some other companies, that it has to offer extras to attract quality personnel. Their stand: "We need to ensure we remain an employer of choice" (Lopez, 1993).

Humility

When partnered with competence, humility unleashes great power in organizations. Humility is not written about much in business literature, yet it is an essential element of giving high-quality service and is very relevant to the customer-interface employee. How can really good service be given unless the employee is willing to be a servant? Putting oneself on a lower level than the customer requires detachment and the New Management Virtue of humility.

Embracing the concept of humility is particularly difficult for old-paradigm managers. It does not fit with the often-accepted image of the strong, tough executive in control. Without a deep and true humility—or former AT&T executive Greenleaf's idea of servant leadership (1977)—managers often unwittingly misuse their power over subordinates. They confuse employee loyalty with obedience and deference, not realizing the deep resentments that such assumptions produce. Later, as the managers' own frustration increases when they realize that their "unimaginative" subordinates have not been telling them about work-related problems, they may angrily say, "But why didn't you bring this to me sooner?" These managers feel a certain self-righteousness towards their "undeserving" people, never understanding how much the managers' own arrogance created their employees' lack of initiative. In order to overcome this usually subconscious expectation of obedience and deference, managers must learn to trust, for "trust flees authority" (Bartholomé and Laurent, 1986).

> Surrender yourself humbly; then you can be trusted to care for all things.

—Lao Tsu, 1989, p. 15

"When is a man loved?"
"When he is without vanity."

—Hindu, *Bhagavad Gita*, 12:13

One company that takes the New Management Virtue of humility and servant leadership seriously is Hewlett-Packard (George Starcher, personal communication, February 1996). If managers focus on their personal interest, subordinates will show low commitment and look to transfer out of the unit. One manager, for example, had the habit of taking credit for what others did and was self-serving. After a restructuring, he was the only one who did not find a new job within H-P, because no other managers wanted him in their unit.

In many organizations, insubordination is not seen in a positive light. At H-P there is an open-door policy, regardless of hierarchical level. If a supervisor puts up roadblocks or discourages subordinates from going over the supervisor's head in cases of conflict, the supervisor's behavior is seen negatively. The company goes a long way to protect this freedom of expression and openness. As a result they can, and do, attract and retain better people than their competitors, there is less resistance to change, and they can pay somewhat less than the competition in exchange for more job security.

He who exalts himself will be humbled and he who humbles himself will be exalted.

—Christian, *The Bible*, Luke 14:11

Lack of Humility

Everyone makes mistakes. Servant leaders can admit wrongdoing and feel genuine remorse for having caused pain to others, while managers enmeshed in ego will have difficulty taking responsibility for their own errors and apologizing with sincerity. This is another reason that selfless love is important in spiritual law and when practicing the New Management Virtues. Because ego and selfless love are basically incompatible, working toward that selflessness helps break through ego.

In business we see examples of dishonest and unscrupulous traders or investors who lose millions of other people's dollars while they themselves end up with millions. The players in the savings and loan debacle demonstrated in court a stunning lack of remorse toward any of the victims who had been defrauded. Millions of dollars were made from leveraged buyouts by managers who then witnessed their own companies being dismantled and thousands losing jobs. There were CEOs who received bonuses of extra millions while their companies were losing money, cutting salaries, and laying off workers.

Then there is the case of the three American auto executives brought in to save the ailing Czech Republic's Tatra truck company, makers of the world's heaviest and most durable trucks (Tully, 1991; "Tatra," 1993; "Czech Privitisation," 1994; Fleet Sheet, 1993; Branegan, 1994; King, 1994; Jaroslav Jirasek, personal communication, January 1995). Under communism, Tatra trucks were one of the Czech Republic's foremost world-class products; they are the only vehicles on the entire planet that can run without supplemental equipment in temperatures as low as minus fifty degrees Celsius (or minus fifty-eight degrees Fahrenheit). Hence, they are the only workable vehicles for such places as the oil fields of Siberia. Tatra suffered heavy losses after the collapse of its biggest market, the Soviet Union and its satellites. In the early days of market reform, everything American seemed magic to the Czechs, who believed that help from the other side of the Atlantic would perform miracles. American consultants and expatriate managers did little to dissuade that unrealistic thinking and had, in fact, their own share of overly optimistic ambitions. In 1993 a contract was made between Tatra and three successful auto and truck executives, with one executive being named as chairman of Tatra's board of directors.

In a country where average personal income is still around $250 per month, these three executives were reportedly paid a collective sum of $120,000 per month for attendance of five days each at the plant (fifteen days total) per month. Then, if there were a successful turnaround (as the Americans seemed confident there would be), they would receive 15 percent of the common stock of the company. Even after the chairman was later appointed to run one of the largest corporations in the United States, he declared that he would be able to fulfill his responsibilities at Tatra at the same time.

After eighteen months, it was clear that what became known as "management by faxing around" was not working, for the company had lost $24 million in 1993 (up from $6.2 million in 1992). The board terminated the contract in September 1994 and was forced to pay a hefty settlement to the three executives.

The Americans' intentions may have been pure in the beginning. In the end, however, they left without any apparent apologies, instead announcing that they expected to finish out the entire contract, blaming losses on "the marketplace" and "the world economy," saying that they had "accomplished a great deal." We may never know the consequences to the executive trio of this situation, but one result for Tatra was a new, extreme caution regarding any technical assistance from Americans. The money spent on the three executives could have been used to hire thirty of the brightest managers from the Czech Republic, or it could have supported three hundred additional workers on the factory floor.

Not every manager is without humility. Odessa College in Odessa, Texas, had an aggressive VP of finance who made millions of dollars for the college during three years trading in derivatives. He apparently had the backing of the administration, including the president, who knew they were in a high-risk game. Finally, in 1994, as rising interest rates knocked the wind out of fixed-income securities, the college lost more than $10 million, which was more than it had earned during the three years of trading. As a result, the college had to slash its operating budget drastically and borrow

another $10 million. It gave early retirement to twenty-two pro-
fessors and, in an unusual move, the president relinquished his
$122,500 salary. Not only did the president seem to exhibit humil-
ity, but evidently the finance VP felt more, for he left the college,
despite the fact that no one had accused him of any wrongdoing
(Knecht, 1994).

Failures such as those just described have a way of increasing
humility for those who are open to understanding their part in the
consequences. By measuring behaviors against spiritual law, humility can result from an awareness of a personal lapse from virtues
such as trustworthiness, unity, respect, and justice, and wisdom can
be gained (Jeffrey Mondschein, personal communication, 1994).

Building Service

Service can be enhanced by managers practicing humility through
taking on the servant-leader role rather than by a more common
leader behavior of assigning everything possible for others to do.
This approach means that the manager is willing to take care of
rather than to be taken care of. Requiring executives and managers
to "work out on the floor," whether it be in the manufacture of
goods or actually working with customers, helps to increase their
appreciation for good service and their sense of selflessness. Exhibit
3.10 lists some of the factors that can build or block service and
humility in an organization, and Exhibit 3.11 can be used to assess
what factors influence service in your company.

An Integrated Approach

We have considered each of the New Management Virtues as individual ideas so that we can more easily describe and discuss them.
In practice, however, a company that operates on the basis of the
New Management Virtues will find that the individual virtues are
interrelated with one another into an integrated, seamless manner
of doing things.

Exhibit 3.10. Factors That May Influence Service in Organizations.

	Builds Service	Blocks Service
Within My Control	1. I try to help those around me whenever I can.	1. Too often I delegate little things to those around me and lose perspective on service, except service to myself.
	2. Sometimes I am able to act as a servant leader.	2. I have been criticized for not apologizing enough when I make mistakes.
Outside My Control	1. Our company encourages managers to work at lower levels for a day periodically in order to understand service and selflessness.	1. Rather than a spirit of service, there are too many attempts to win the boss's approval.
		2. Some managers are filled with too much ego and tend to be self-serving.

Exhibit 3.11. What Factors Influence Service in My Company?

	Builds Service	Blocks Service
Within My Control		
Outside My Control		

For example, control management and command decision making—the old paradigm—are based on domination. They are being replaced, however, with the new paradigm concepts of commitment leadership and consensus decisions, which require not only unity, so that the workers will be committed, but also trust, so that workers will feel confident enough to speak out during group discussions. Shifting to a team structure, which has the potential for producing outstanding work, requires respect and dignity, for without such qualities the result will be on the order of Groupthink or a collectivistic team with all members thinking nearly alike.

Or consider the New Management Virtue of service and humility. In order to have humility, managers must trust more. One way of creating trust is to behave in a more trustworthy manner, as well as to treat each person with justice and dignity. If subordinates sense injustice and disrespect, trust will evaporate. To develop humility, it is essential also to develop trustworthiness, justice, and respect.

In the next chapter we will look in some detail at how these New Management Virtues work in practice for managers and organizations.

> *He who possesses character and discrimination, who is just, speaks the truth, and does what is his own business, him the world will hold dear.*
>
> —Buddhist, *The Dhammapada*, 217
> (1965, p. 34)

Chapter Four

The New Management Virtues at Work

⁐

It is from understanding that power comes.
—*Black Elk, American Indian mystic*

The most important human endeavor is the striving
for morality in our actions. Our inner balance and
even our very existence depend on it. Only
morality in actions give beauty and dignity to life.
—*Albert Einstein*

Just as individuals can grow spiritually, so can companies. In this
chapter I share stories of some organizations that are applying the
spiritual laws and the New Management Virtues. They include
U.S. companies, as well as one in Brazil. Some of the companies
have spiritual practices without calling them by that name, while
two of them are openly and intentionally founded on spirituality.
Each company described has its own way of being spiritual, with
strengths shown in different areas.

"God Is My Reference Point"

At least one enormously successful company is unabashedly based on
spirituality. Chairman C. William Pollard believes that honoring
God is the best management principle around, and he sees God as
his point of reference. He knows that his company, which has grown
from a local rug-cleaning business to a $4 billion a year operation

89

with 36,000 employees, needs a unifying force. For ServiceMaster, it is a belief in God (Young, 1994; Dubashi, 1994).

ServiceMaster has gone at least one step further than merely looking at the New Management Virtue of unity. This company manages hospitals and nursing homes; fills residential needs through its pest, lawn (TruGreen-ChemLawn), and cleaning divisions (Merry Maids); and provides custodial, food service, and grounds management to educational institutions. It has "unity in diversity" as its theme and one of its main goals. Unlike some other organizations that speak the ideology of diversity but do not truly internalize its concepts, ServiceMaster is committed to making real corporate-level changes. Management feels that having diversity can be an asset to the company, if each person's contribution is seen as worthy and the company is able to harness the differences in people. This is quite different from the more traditional approaches that see diversity as a process of the minority group learning to assimilate itself into the majority (Cantu, 1994).

Does this philosophy work? If we look at the material evidence of the company's success, evidently it does. During 1993, the ServiceMaster's revenues were $3.9 billion, with net income up 20 percent from the previous year. In 1994, profits were up another 21 percent, with an astonishing 45 percent increase in the consumer services division. Nineteen ninety-four was the twenty-fourth consecutive year of growth in revenue and profits. During this entire period, revenue has grown (compounded rate) 19 percent and profit, 22 percent. The company has continued to increase its client base and has an impressive return on investment. Income continued to increase by 25 percent in 1995 (ServiceMaster, 1996). Currently ServiceMaster is ranked within the top 5 percent of New York Stock Exchange companies for consistency in distribution and dividend payments to shareholders (ServiceMaster, 1994, 1995a; Henkoff, 1992).

ServiceMaster is not content with only material advances. It also tries to give something back to the community. As a result, in June 1994 it received an award as a "Green Chip" company, citing its ability to combine a healthy financial picture with social vision, including corporate mission, environmental impact, employee empowerment, and community relations.

With this remarkable record, one could expect that being profitable was the number one goal of ServiceMaster. Not so, according to its corporate objectives, which are, in order of priority: "to honor God in all we do, to help people develop, to pursue excellence, and to grow profitably" (Cantu, 1994, p. 9).

ServiceMaster maintains that the first two goals are the real end goals and the last two are means to the end. How different this is from what is considered the norm or, in fact, from what is believed to be the essential role of business, that is, to increase shareholder wealth. And yet, with profitability as the last of their four goals, ServiceMaster has been able to be more than mildly successful for the past twenty-four years.

A further look at the first goal indicates the spiritual foundation upon which the company seems to rest. Indeed, the first page of every annual report includes a quotation from the Old Testament, such as 1994's: "God saw all that He had made, and it was very good" (Genesis 1:31).

Building Relationships

> We view our reputation [for integrity as] as important an asset to our business as the high technologies that we develop and bring to our marketplace [Skooglund, 1994, p. 1].

Texas Instruments (TI) is a high-tech manufacturer of semiconductors. It has revenues of about $10 billion and 60,000 employees in thirty countries.

TI owes much of it success to the New Management Virtue of trustworthiness, as demonstrated by its proactive approach to ethics and morality. Ethics director Carl Skooglund told me that TI was one of the first companies to develop a code of ethics (in 1961), and has held itself to high standards of integrity and openness (personal communication, December 1994). Still, in the 1980s, TI's leaders were concerned about all of the corruption, court cases, and prison sentences that involved U.S. executives and managers, and that in a company as large and complex as TI, unless more dramatic measures were taken to ensure the integration of TI's ethics by the many employees worldwide, there was danger of erosion of TI's moral foundation. Employees were then and are now in a rapidly changing environment where many difficult decisions have to be made daily that are close calls with no clear right or wrong answer. Even in the 1980s, people trusted TI, and TI's management wanted to keep it that way. "People want to do business with those they can trust," says Skooglund (1994, p. 2), and trust is clearly the foundation for all solid business relationships. "Trust is established only when there is a reputation for ethics and integrity. When we deal with one another openly and honestly, it enables us to gain the most from our relationships."

TI's ethics office was born in 1987 with a threefold purpose. The first purpose was to define expectations and requirements. The second was to communicate these ethical principles by as many vehicles as possible, including booklets and a weekly news article that went out on the electronic mail system to 30,000 terminals worldwide. Topics of these articles have included how to determine whether a gift is acceptable, how to make patent awards in other countries, proper information exchange, how to deal with chain letters, the many faces of theft, including software copying, and so on. More recently, the ethics office has produced a series of more than fifty short (less than five-minute) videotapes on ethical dilemmas, which managers can play for employees as a means to develop discussion.

The third purpose was to create a feedback network. Any TI employee who has a question or concern can (anonymously if desired) call a toll-free number in the United States or Canada, send a message to a separate U.S. post office box, or communicate through a secure and confidential terminal connected to the 30,000 other terminals. At present the ethics office receives about

120 calls a month, mostly from people with preventive questions about what to do in certain situations.

So powerful is TI's commitment to maintaining this trust and integrity that it has sometimes gone the extra, and unneeded, mile to ensure the proper outcome. After the products had been delivered on one of its contracts, TI told the procurement officer that a slight technical variation had been noticed, which had an infinitesimal chance of affecting successful use of the product. The product had been carefully manufactured to contractual requirements. Because of the small potential for problems, TI paid at great loss for the product to be recalled and adjusted. The procurement officer was pleasantly surprised. He said he was unable to watch over every aspect of a contractor's performance, but that in the future he would always trust TI to do the right thing, no matter what. Compare this with the near-scandal in recent years of Intel and its Pentium chip, which was found to have some minor imperfections that would only affect users needing to perform complex mathematical computations. Intel initially said it would only replace the chip to users that Intel deemed needed perfection. Later, as a result of public outcry, Intel said it would replace the chip for anyone. Intel's reputation has not been enhanced by this incident.

A company that wants to be proud of its ethical standards of integrity, says Skooglund, needs to keep three things in mind. If any of the three is absent, efforts will be perceived as without substance and merely symbolic. In this model, leaders must

1. *Define ethical expectations* relentlessly and forcefully.

2. *Lead by personal example*, for it is the leaders' actions and behaviors that speak the loudest. If there is a gap between espoused theory and the practice of management, credibility will be lost. Making the right call is a powerful action, even if it means a loss in short-term profits, but it is an action that demonstrates a commitment to do the right thing in the long run. Such role modeling is helpful. One employee wrote, "It is

easier to work in an organization [in which] you know if you make the right call but a tough call, you will be supported."

3. *Open up lines of communication,* so that everyone feels free to offer thoughts, opinions, and ideas. More important, employees must believe they can bring up problems without fear of punishment or retribution. Often it is the bad news that leaders need most to make informed decisions.

What about hard times? I asked Skooglund, because all of this works much easier when a company is in prosperous times. He related to me what happened when TI lost much of its previous business in defense contracting, which had amounted to 30 percent of its total business. Cutbacks were necessary, but how to do them in an ethical and caring manner? First, employees were often placed somewhere else in the company, or else strong severance packages were given. TI's managers behaved differently from managers who use "normal" business practices, in which information on layoffs is closely held until the last minute. Around this time, rumors of the true situation are often denied in order to avoid what is expected, namely, employee slough-off after the pink slip is received. An early notification program such as TI's obliges management to let employees know as soon as "surplus jobs" are identified, sometimes up to a year before the layoff will occur. TI can no longer offer the promise of permanent or even long-term employment for good service, because business conditions change too rapidly. "We don't control our market," he said. However, TI invests heavily in employee training and development, not only to help the company but also to make sure that employees become more employable. Executives also seem to have a sensitivity to others during hard times. In the midst of a severe layoff, management decided to keep in storage some new and already paid-for furniture, in order not to create more hurt and resentment. Contrast this with IBM. At the same time that it was laying off several thousand employees (in effect, laying off several thousand families), it was also negotiating a compensation package to new CEO Louis Gerstner of $3.5 million in annual pay plus a one-time bonus of $5 million and 500,000 stock options (Vogl, 1993).

Resources invested in developing ethical and moral foundations have paid off at TI. Employees have told people in the ethics office that they were proud to work for a company that holds them to the highest standards. The ethics office also learned that most workers, given the appropriate resources and support, want to do the right thing, all of which helps keep TI "clean." As Skooglund (1994, p. 1) said, "We understand that a reputation for integrity is something that cannot be purchased. It must be earned over a long period of time."

The Executive Poet

Work can provide the opportunity for spiritual and personal, as well as financial, growth. If it doesn't we are wasting far too much of our lives on it.

Management is, in fact, a sacred trust in which the well-being of other people is put into your care during most of their waking hours.

—James Autry, 1991, pp. 13, 15

Few would assume that these words were from the president of a large and successful organization. Autry rose from writer to copyeditor to manager to, finally, president of the Meredith Magazine Group, which publishes *Better Homes & Gardens* and *Ladies' Home Journal*, and is a $500 million operation with nine hundred employees.

Even with such an impressive background, Autry still gets criticized for being naive. When people make such an accusation, he says, it means they see the person as "too trusting" or "not paranoid enough." He believes the best policy is to trust everyone and to "presume goodwill," for these are the most productive and rewarding attitudes possible. Will some people take advantage? Yes, but these usually are the ones who do substandard work, who get "found out" in other ways. Autry is big on trust. Without trust, you can't get employees to do much.

Who does not trust enough will not be trusted.

—Lao Tsu, 1989, p. 19

And yet, what do most companies do? Management thinks up many ways to let employees feel they are not trusted (such as excessive controls; questioning them on their use of funds, expense accounts, and sick days; being suspiciousness of long lunch hours and coffee breaks, and extra days taken on business trips), and there are even managers who devote significant portions of their careers to "all that trivia" (Autry, 1991, p. 125), with a predictable result: when employees are not treated as trustworthy, they do not feel trusted, and ultimately they do not trust management. It is the Wisdom of Love again, showing us the natural consequences of being treated as untrustworthy.

Quit being a cop and start being a manager, a motivator, Autry says. Let people know you trust them by taking them at face value, by believing them, by expecting that they will get the work done. Isn't that how managers want to be treated by their own bosses?

Being trustworthy, of course, requires honesty, which is always the best policy, asserts Autry. However, under the guise of honesty, many times managers rationalize tactlessness. They believe this to be more efficient. Because such ineffective behavior requires brutality, it saves time but damages relationships, which in the end is always inefficient.

Love and caring are foundations of Autry's management style, and he finds it incomprehensible to think of management sans caring, which is quite opposite to the prevailing view. Rather than boasting about how the company was run on such well-developed technologies and principles, Autry preferred to emphasize how they relied on the power of the human heart.

Autry also discovered that patience paid off in the end. Instead of pushing ideas on people, managers achieved better results when they trusted that employees would come to the ideas themselves, even if it took longer. In the end, trusting employees was more effective, because the ideas thus became *the employees' ideas*, and they predictably put more energy into the outcomes. This approach often required great patience on the part of management, who "knew" they were right.

Trust at TDI

TDIndustries, a mechanical contracting and service firm in Dallas that was founded in 1946, almost went under in 1989 (Liebig, 1994). It survived due to the devotion of the 750 employees and the company's long-term culture of mutual trust, training and development, communication, and employee ownership. These values are not hollow. TDI was listed by Levering and Moskowitz (1993) as one of the one hundred best American companies to work for. Some interviewers have asked TDI what kinds of programs it has used to create such a high level of trust. When TDI answered that it used information on profit-sharing, all-day meetings between the owner and groups of twenty employees, removal of management perks, active implementation of worker participation, intense and sincere focus on quality and innovation, this answer was not enough. The interviewers wanted to know about the trust-building programs—Why was TDI regarded as trustworthy by employees? A TDI manager's response was, "Because it *is*. It *is* a trustworthy company. New employees (called TDPartners) receive a value statement on leadership, which includes statements that leaders (a) are first a servant of those they lead . . . (b) do not say, 'Get going.' Instead they say, 'Let's go!' (c) assume their followers are working with them . . . and that they share in the reward . . . (d) are people builders, (e) use their heart as well as their head . . . (f) can be led. They are not interested in having their own way, but in finding the best way" (Liebig, 1994, p. 106).

Unlike most mission statements, TDI's begins with concern for employee development (TDIndustries, 1994): "We are committed

to providing outstanding career opportunities by exceeding our customers' expectations through continuous aggressive improvement."
Key managers at TDI met in late 1993 to determine a vision of the
future. One strategy to achieve their goals of business growth and
profitability was to "focus on fewer customers so they can serve
them better" (Lowes, 1994). Imagine a company intentionally
reducing its customer base in order to more effectively take care of
customer needs. It speaks not only to building trust but to regarding service as one of the company's highest strategies. How does
this strategy translate into practical help for customers? In one
example, TDI's project for East Texas Baptist University resulted in
about a 28 percent reduction in energy costs for the university
("New Energy Saving System," 1993).

The Wisdom of Love would tell us that trust is not possible
without upper levels being trustworthy and without top management sharing information with lower levels, avoiding secrecy
and collusion. "Openness is the action manifestation of trust. If
the system isn't open, don't talk about trust," says Jacques Chaize,
managing director of SOCIA in France (Liebig, 1994, p. 113).
Chaize's ideas mirror the European Business Ethics Network's
stated values, including not only trust and openness but also transparency. Similar to openness, transparency brings information out
in the open, prevents secrecy, and helps to establish deep and
long-lasting trust.

Justice at Hewlett-Packard

Part of Hewlett-Packard's (H-P) folklore is a story about leadership
in the company, and it says a great deal about what the company
stands for. Some years ago it came to the attention of H-P management that a purchasing agent had just shrewdly negotiated a
contract at a price much lower than normal for H-P. Naturally, the
agent was quite proud of his accomplishment. After management
heard that the price did not allow the supplier any profit, an immediate call was made to the supplier. After confirming the facts,

management renegotiated a new and "fair" price that allowed both sides reasonable profit. Because of H-P's concern for the New Management Virtue of justice, the groundwork was laid for a long and fruitful relationship. This supplier has consistently gone out of its way to provide impeccable quality, timely delivery, and suggestions on product improvements. That is, it has become a real partner to H-P, ultimately helping it to become more profitable.

Just the opposite has occurred at General Motors (GM), which had a cost-cutting drive in recent years and tightened the screws on suppliers to drive down costs to the bare bones. As a result, GM is having quality problems, receiving customer complaints, and so on as their suppliers assign better engineers to other customers with whom they can collaborate more profitably and fairly (George Starcher, personal communication, September 1995). GM's cost slasher par excellance was Jose Ignacio Lopez de Arriortua—the "Grand Inquisitor" (Jenkins, 1996, p. 6)—who ripped up contracts and ignored agreements with suppliers, knowing they would succumb to this colossal customer. Even before his troubles at VW (where he was virtually forced out in late 1996) he was referred to as a betrayer. GM headquarters didn't seem to mind, since he did cut $2 billion in his three hundred days on the job. By the time he left GM, diminishing returns were already starting to appear; Oldsmobile and Cadillac assembly lines were thrown into disarray because a low-cost supplier could not deliver.

Hewlett-Packard embodies others of the New Management virtues as well (Hewlett-Packard, 1989). Their organizational requirements include having

1. "Trust and respect for individuals" (p. 2). They attract highly capable and innovative people throughout the organization and offer them opportunities to increase their knowledge and skills (respect and dignity).

2. Objectives and leadership that "generate enthusiasm" (p. 2) at all levels (respect and dignity; service).

3. Uncompromising integrity and honesty in all its affairs; any-thing less than the highest standards of business ethics is unacceptable (trustworthiness).

4. All levels working in unison toward company objectives, understanding that efficiency and achievement can only be obtained through effective cooperative effort (unity).

How do the New Management Virtues work in practice at H-P? Here are a few examples of the outcomes. First, H-P has a wide reputation for honesty and trustworthiness in customs declara-tions. As a result, there is much less inspection of H-P shipments, resulting in faster expediting of clearance and delivery time, and lower cost.

H-P has a good corporate citizenship policy and a history of philanthropy. It regularly gives state-of-the-art equipment to edu-cational institutions and funds nonprofit organizations, particularly in the areas of math and science education. At the local level, H-P donated a significant amount of money to the county swimming pool where the headquarters is located; it is also active with the schools, and so on. As a result, the community will buy H-P prod-ucts over the competition, and H-P can retain and recruit the best people more easily. Employees like to know that their employer cares about the community.

But so what? What do these values do in the marketplace? Do all these policies and virtues really help H-P to be more successful? Yes, at least under present conditions.

Ten years ago, H-P, the inventor of handheld calculators, had to retreat out of that business due to Japan's cheaper and well-designed units. Similarly, in 1985, Japan made 80 percent of all computer printers that Americans bought, and *The Wall Street Journal* called that market "the stronghold of Japanese industry." Through savvy corporate restructuring founded on the previously mentioned virtues, on innovation, on entrepreneurship, and on rejection of the "rugged individualism of cowboy culture" (Yoder, 1994, p. 7), H-P gained its lost market and sold about $8 billion of printers in 1993, which is greater than Hollywood's yearly box-office revenues. H-P currently holds 55 percent of the inkjet printer world market (Yoder, 1994).

The company didn't achieve such a turnaround by using high-handed tactics or sophisticated financial maneuvers; by cutting corners, abusing, or taking advantage of employees; or by using power plays in the office. H-P succeeded by hiring and retaining smart people, treating them well, encouraging them, rewarding risk takers, and always being trustworthy.

Let Companies Be Ruled by Wisdom

It's not socialist. . . . It isn't purely capitalistic, either. It is a new way.
A third way. A more human, trusting, productive, exhilarating, and,
in every sense, rewarding way [Semler, 1993, p. ix].

Ricardo Semler took over the moribund Semco from his father in 1980 and immediately began a change program. Over the course of several years, he completely transformed the company, which is now the largest marine and food-processing machinery manufacturer in Brazil. This transformation was accomplished by "refusing to squander [their] greatest resource, [their] people" (1993, p. 7). Semco is a company in which employees are expected to perform well and to act in a trustworthy manner. In short, Semler treats employees with respect and dignity.

His methods are based on participation, profit sharing, and information. By turning over most power to his employees, Semler has catapulted his company into incredible growth in revenues over ten years, despite incredibly harsh and unpredictable economic conditions in Brazil. At Semco there are no secretaries, no walls, no set hours or dress codes. Managers determine their own salaries and are evaluated regularly by subordinates, who fill out an inventory; the results are posted on bulletin boards. The company's books are open to anyone, anytime (all workers are offered courses in reading balance sheets and cash-flow statements). Workers share in 22 percent of the profits. Managers do their own faxing, phoning, and fetching of guests. Sounds crazy, doesn't it? Most people would see such a situation as chaos (Semler, 1994).

Yet Semco has shown increases since 1980 of 700 percent in productivity and 500 percent in profit, with sales volume increasing from $4 million to $20 million. In addition, there is little turnover at Semco, and the list of job applicants is two thousand people long.

At Semco, people are self-propelled, instead of being pushed forward. They are encouraged to communicate openly and honestly, and then not punished for that, as some companies do in a more typical doublespeak. Semler's management model seriously challenges the accepted and often unquestioned pyramid view of corporations. Without knowing the financial health of Semco, most would say it couldn't work.

Why do they say this? As Semler says, they do not expect their employees to want to come to work late or leave early, or to work as minimally as possible. After all, these same workers raise children, belong to the PTA, elect governmental officials, and so on.

Semler's values of respect and dignity come through in the following statement (Semler, 1993, p. 59): "They are adults. At Semco, we treat them like adults. We trust them. We don't make our employees ask permission to go to the bathroom, or have security guards check them as they leave for the day. We get out of their way and let them do their jobs."

Our Clients' Success Is Our Success

"I believe the importance of business is to create meaningful work through meeting customer needs, to employ committed people, and to make a profit. In that order!" declared Robert Rosenfeld, president and founder of Idea Connection Systems, a management consulting business concerned with sustaining innovation in organizations (personal communication, January 1995). Rosenfeld said that his company sees spirituality and business as compatible concepts. You *can* be spiritual and also make a profit. But the most important thing, he emphasized, is to do good.

When Rosenfeld began Idea Connection Systems, he followed three central principles:

1. To do something with a positive social impact—to do good.

2. To create something that would outlive the company; therefore money was not the main force.

3. To build a company where employees would have to be told to go home.

The last principle fascinated me and I asked more about it. Vice president Michael Winger-Bearskin (personal communication, January 1995) said that principle affected every behavior in the company. It had to be a place that people wanted to be, both physically and emotionally. The work had to be challenging, in a way that the made employees feel like a central part of the force for social change—that they, too, had a role in the change. Hiring employees whose values aligned with this principle became very important. If employees did not have these values, they would have a problem meeting clients' needs.

Rosenfeld told of a recent incident that illustrates how this value alignment influences the high levels of motivation by employees. Some clients were due in from the Netherlands but could only come on Sunday. Don Braun, who is the all-around maintenance, shipping, and receiving person for Idea Connection Systems, took the initiative to make the clients feel at home. Unknown to Rosenfeld, Braun arrived early Sunday morning, made coffee, brought in fresh pastries and tidied up the offices, then went home. When Rosenfeld arrived to meet the clients, he thought the coffee would be cold and leftover and was surprised to see that it was fresh. Braun did this on his own because he knew it was important to show such hospitality. "This kind of commitment has to translate all the way down the organization in order for it to be truly successful, in order for us to fill clients' needs the way we think is important."

This commitment results because the company is based on an explicit set of values translated into the New Management Virtues of respect, trust, dignity, and service. "We have the assumption that people are here to do what is right," said Rosenfeld. The company's respect extends not only to its employees but also to its customers.

"We believe the relationships we build are more important than the business we get," both Rosenfeld and Winger-Bearskin told me. "This has been our core value from day one. We have a confidence that if we build these relationships the business will happen." Rosenfeld told me that the company befriends its clients, who become part of the Idea Connection Systems family. Some clients prefer to stay at Rosenfeld's house rather than at a hotel when they visit the company's offices in Rochester, New York.

Rosenfeld and Winger-Bearskin reminisced about the early years, the difficulties of getting started. They wondered, back in 1988, if they could make it. They sat in the basement of Rosenfeld's house, where their office originally was, and discussed the sacrifices both had made to start the business and how their families were all at risk. "I'll give it until next year," Winger-Bearskin said. "If it doesn't take off, then I'll have to go and get back to a regular job again." Within a few months they had landed a huge contract with a Fortune 100 company.

Now, some nine years later, they have seventy-eight employees in four branches in the United States and Europe. Twenty of their many clients have been listed in the Fortune 100. In the past four years they have increased their revenues by more than 40 percent each year and have increased the number of employees more than 100 percent in the past year alone. A few years ago they brought in another partner, David DeMarco, whose skills complement those of Rosenfeld and Winger-Bearskin. Because of their emphasis on serving their clients and developing relationships, they have been able to maintain a presence in more than 80 percent of all the companies they have ever worked with. An example of the kind of commitment they get from clients is a Fortune 100 company that during the recent recession cut back all of its outside vendors, with one exception: Idea Connection Systems.

Another New Management Virtue the company operates with is justice. In order to determine how much to charge a client, employees do role plays, with someone representing Idea Connection Systems and someone else representing the client, in order to make sure that needs are met on both sides. Even though client needs are paramount, the company realizes that there must be a balance. If they are only concerned with client needs and not those of the company, they would end up shortchanging the business.

Because so much of the business is based on cognitive (how we think) and conative (what we do) behaviors, part of the culture has become a continual self- and group-reflection on what it means to be different. A continuous dynamic discussion is ongoing at all levels of the organization. "It is embedded behavior," said Winger-Bearskin.

One of the most important insights Winger-Bearskin has gained during these years is an understanding of the prime difference between publicly held and privately held companies. Idea Connection Systems has worked with several family-owned companies, including Milliken, S. C. Johnson and Sons, and Hallmark, in which varying degrees of control are exerted by the founding families. In the private companies, Winger-Bearskin told me, you can go to any employee at any level. They all share a common feeling, that no matter how good or bad their own managers are, they believe in their hearts that they can go to the family and the family will listen to them. And they are right. Even if the families are not actively running the company, they still see it as their role to guard the spirit of the company.

"My question is," asked Winger-Bearskin, "in a public company, who is there to take care of the spirit of the organization?"

Consultation

Rosenfeld and Winger-Bearskin attribute much of the success of Idea Connection Systems to the company's use, from the very beginning, of a decision-making process known as *consultation*, in which synergy is achieved through utilizing the best of each team member. This process predates the similar and more popular process known as *dialogue*. Consultation is based on the New Management Virtues of trustworthiness, respect, dignity, and unity.

Without the emphasis on consultation, Idea Connection Systems probably would not have grown as it has. In the beginning, the structure was designed to have the management team work towards consensus on all decisions. If this did not work out, then Rosenfeld was to make the final decision. So, much time is spent consulting and discussing issues and working toward understanding each other. After nine years, Rosenfeld has never had to make a major decision alone.

Consultation obligates all persons to speak their minds, while at the same time respecting the dignity of the others in the group. Its goal is to search for the best solution while both creating unity and enhancing the unique contributions of each member.

Idea Connection Systems is firmly based on the concept of unity in diversity and works to practice that in every way, believing consultation to be a prime force. Since much of the business is helping organizations to sustain innovation, Idea Connection Systems believes it must also leverage diversity for maximum innovation.[1]

Consultation requires anyone who speaks to do so not with an attitude of correctness but rather with the idea of contributing to consensus. While listening, each person needs to carefully consider the merits of what is being put forth (listening with respect), rather than automatically thinking of ways to oppose or undermine the argument. If another idea seems worthy, the listener should accept it and not willfully hold on to his or her own (see Exhibit 4.1).

Exhibit 4.1. Consultation: Turning Conjecture into Certainty.

Purpose
- Create team commitment, trust among diverse participants
- Identify opportunities and solve problems
- Determine the best course of action

Ten Principles for Success
1. Respect each participant and appreciate each other's diversity. This is the prime requisite for consultation.
2. Value and consider all contributions. Belittle none. Withhold evaluation until sufficient information has been gathered.*
3. Contribute and express opinions with complete freedom.
4. Carefully consider the views of others—if a valid point of view has been offered, accept it as your own.
5. Keep to the mission at hand. Extraneous conversation may be important to team building, but it is not consultation, which is solution driven.
6. Share in the group's unified purpose—desire for success of the mission.
7. Expect the truth to emerge from the clash of differing opinions. Optimum solutions emerge from diversity of opinion.
8. Once stated, let go of opinions. Don't try to "defend" your position, but rather let it go. Ownership causes disharmony among the team and almost always gets in the way of finding the truth.
9. Contribute to maintaining a friendly atmosphere by speaking with courtesy, dignity, care, and moderation. This will promote unity and openness.
10. Seek consensus. But if consensus is impossible, let the majority rule. Remember, though, that decisions, once made, become the decision of every participant. After the group has decided, dissenting opinions are destructive to the success of the mission. When decisions are undertaken with total group support, wrong decisions can be more fully observed and corrected.

*Harley Training & Consulting, Inc., of Minneapolis has further developed this concept by developing a model whose steps alternately apply and suspend critical judgment.

Source: Robert Rosenfeld and Michael Winger-Bearskin, © 1989 Idea Connection Systems, Inc. All rights reserved.

Consultation has three main features:

1. Meeting group goals (unity)
2. Utilizing diversity in order to discover the best solution
3. Respect of others' ideas, so that no one is ever belittled

The principles underlying this process are (1) purity of motive, (2) truth seeking, (3) patience and courtesy, and (4) unity. These principles are related to the New Management Virtues of trustworthiness, respect, dignity, and unity.

Consultation requires group members to value contributions from all members without invoking hierarchy in the decision-making process. Striving to make one's opinions dominant is too often the case in normal discussions, where leadership gets confused with domination. Consultation requires full participation of all members, and leadership is expressed in the New Management Virtue of service to the group.

Consultation is propelled by goals that are formed by the sincere collective will of individuals and made successful by the integration of differences within a framework of unity. This is consultation's key element—unity of thought and action emerge from an acceptance of difference, not from its negation.

The three main features of consultation—meeting group goals, utilizing diversity, and maintaining respect—are all central to innovation in an organization. Consultation as a process can soften the rigidity of a corporate structure, allowing ideas to navigate successfully through a complex system.

Consultation in Action

An example of how potent these features are comes from Judge Dorothy Nelson (1994), who serves on the United States Court of Appeals in the nine western states:

The principle of consultation has very practical applications. A high rate of crime resulted in seventeen or eighteen arrests a day in one California high school. At that time we had a neighborhood Justice Center where we were teaching people the art of mediation, which is a form of consultation. We trained four of the gang leaders in the art of consultation or mediation.

I called up the police chief and asked him to come to the library and engage in mediation with some students of the high school. After asking, "Why should I?" he finally agreed. As they had been trained to do, the students and mediators sat around this simple little table and said, "Mr. Police Chief, what do you think the problems are? What do you think the facts are?" His response had to do with not enough police, not enough patrol cars, etc.

Then they said, "Let us tell you what we think the problems are. School closes at 2:30 in the afternoon, the gates are locked, we're not permitted on school grounds, there are no jobs for high school students in this community, so what's a teenager going to do? They're going to get into trouble."

"Well, Mr. Police Chief, what do you think the solutions are?" More police, more patrol cars, higher fences, etc. The students' solutions were: unlock the gates, put two policemen inside, let us get teacher sponsors for after-school sports, arts, drama, etc.

Well, I wouldn't tell you this story unless it had worked. In one year the arrests went down from seventeen or eighteen a day to three or four a month. I had the four student leaders to my chambers for lunch. I asked one fifteen-year-old boy, "Edward, what did you think of all this?"

And Edward told me, "First of all, I thought the police chief was nicer than I thought he would be. Secondly," he said, "you know, Judge, I'm fifteen, and I hadn't had a decent conversation with my father since I was twelve. I went home and I said, 'Dad, let's mediate our disputes.' And afterward I talked to him about listening and agreeing on the facts and talking about what the issues were and what principles ought to apply and applying them, and you know, I had the first decent conversation with my dad that I'd had since I was twelve."

This is the power of consultation. It is the most powerful tool. Edward had shown that he could take those principles he'd learned

to deal with his school problems into his family life. Those principles apply in the community [and] the nation, and [at] the international level.

Judge Nelson's example shows how consultation is solution driven as opposed to power oriented. Avoided are power plays or asser-
tions of rightness from authority. The goal is to investigate the truth.

Spirit and Fear

The true spirit of consultation requires a spiritual atmosphere, otherwise it is likely to have a hollowness to it, and to fall prey to personal agendas. It requires a fear-*less* atmosphere, for only in that
context can participants be fully open and frank about their ideas.
Fear is one of the greatest diseases of mankind, and it is rampant in
organizations and in group decision making because power has often
become an entity in itself instead of a tool for living. People use
power, sometimes in the form of factual knowledge, to dominate
others rather than as a means of facilitating processes. Honesty has
lost its identity, with courtesy and respect seen as something of a
hindrance to group expression. Ego, a sense of competition, and our
tendency to attack almost everything we do not understand, prevent us from utilizing fully the potential of all members.

> *There is no fear in love; but perfect love casteth out fear:*
> *because fear hath torment. He that feareth is not made perfect*
> *in love.*

> —Christian, *The Bible*, 1 John 4:18

In order for consultation to really work, behaviors are required
that build on the New Management Virtues: purity of motive,
respect, lack of ego, intention to forget self-interest, humility,
respect and courtesy, as well as radiance of spirit, which means
courage to care for and trust what is happening and to encourage
others to find new ways of thinking.

Spirituality at Work

Ben & Jerry's Ice Cream has had such phenomenal growth and success because of their commitment to quality and their underlying corporate philosophy that incorporates the New Management Virtues of trustworthiness and justice.[2] Toyota has gained respect in the marketplace because of the trust customers have in its quality. Similarly, Harley-Davidson achieved a corporate miracle turn-around by using simple principles of quality, justice, and respect to employees in its new organization structure and decision-making system.

In short, spirituality is not incompatible with market gains. However, one cannot "get spiritual" in order to be more profitable. The material gains come as a side effect of the spirituality, or of the move toward solid trustworthiness and justice. Otherwise we are still in the materialistic spirituality mode. All of the world's religions teach the importance of pure intentions and egoless devotion to virtuous behavior. Positive effects are largely due to the selflessness of the acts.

Chapter Five

Acting with the Wisdom of Love

᎒

The power of Love, as the basis of [an organization]
has never been tried. . . . There will always be [rule]
of force where men are selfish.

—*Ralph Waldo Emerson,*

A coward is incapable of exhibiting love; it is the
prerogative of the brave.

—*Mahatma Gandhi*

Much of the effort in organizational change that we have seen in
recent years has a short half-life of real usefulness to the company.
One statistic is worth repeating: the failure rate of change efforts
tops 50 percent (Hammer and Champy, 1993). Because the changes
do not go deep enough, to the emotional or spiritual levels, the
efforts often do not take.

Thus we come back full circle to our starting part in this book.
If what we are currently doing to create change is not working,
what should we do instead?

What is needed is fundamental transformation in the foundation (the roots) of the organization. Until that foundation is transformed into one with more justice, dignity, service, trustworthiness,
and love, all the strategies, slogans, and training programs in the
world will not help.

This kind of fundamental change cannot be achieved by simply teaching new behaviors or new practices. First and foremost, we
need to change the mindset of workers (Covey, 1989b). If people

are managed with principles, rather than merely skills, they can figure out how to handle unusual situations without violating those principles.

Real change, then, requires going to the roots of the organization as well as addressing the way people think. In order for the rubber band not to snap back, there must be systemic changes in values and spirit—and love. These principles are then translated into behaviors based on the New Management Virtues. And that is where we find difficulty.

My colleague Robin Lawton, a successful consultant on changing corporate culture (Lawton, 1993; personal communication, 1996), told me that most managers he works with are really interested in bringing meaning into work, in creating a culture based on higher values. They understand what this means and how important it is for the workplace. In fact, they often tell him that the lack of meaning and values is the cause of many problems managers have. When Lawton asks managers how they operationalize their desire for deeper values and more meaning, they look at him with blank stares. In short, they see the need but they can't quite implement a solution.

Operationalizing Spirituality

Knowing that determining *what* is needed is far different from being able to lay out the *how* and from having the *will* to do it. How to operationalize the New Management Virtues and spirituality is often the really tricky question, and the point where many managers get stuck. Because such transformation is neither easy to do nor lends itself to a quick fix, making such transformations requires real commitment. Bringing about effective and enduring change in values and culture in an organization is a long-term process.

There are no tricks, no secrets, no formulas for bringing love, spirituality, and the New Management Virtues into organizations.

You can't just go to a seminar and suddenly "get spiritual." A change in focus of this magnitude requires commitment and time.

Embrascon is a highly successful management consulting firm in Brazil. It works with companies to help them experience transformation and improve their human processes such as integration, communication, innovation, and participation (Liebig, 1994). Jose Affonso Fausto Barbosa, president of the company, told me that in order for companies to develop in love and spirituality, they must address power issues because most unethical behaviors in the workplace result from power abuses (personal communication, November 22, 1994).

After twenty years in the field, Fausto Barbosa has found the following:

1. Organizational transformation is in reality human transformation in the workplace, for the company is really a group of people.
2. The success of the process depends on the top executive's transformation.
3. A process such as this shouldn't be done in less than two years, with three years preferable.
4. At the end, about 30 percent of the participants will be transformed to some degree, 50 percent will be open to future experiences but not yet transformed, and about 20 percent will be against the transformation process or simply will not care.

Do these ideas work? Since Embrascon began applying them to engineering projects, the company has saved clients about 40 percent of their preconstruction estimated costs, which now total over $600 million (Liebig, 1994). This is accomplished through long consultation sessions in which group process is allowed to develop and each person faces their own potential. As part of the procedure, each employee is made aware of his or her own part in achieving the company mission. Fausto Barbosa believes that this is the best way to unleash human potential, for "we have everything inside us. I'm telling people nothing. I am energizing what is already there" (Liebig, 1994, p. 100).

A time frame of two to three years is not unique. Jim Autry (personal communication, December 1995) told me he has been working with a company in Sydney, Australia, for almost three years, and it has taken that whole time to achieve real transformation. From the beginning his goal was to create a sense of community, which he accomplished through open communication. He said that most of us spend 95 to 98 percent of our time on logistics, even with those closest to us, such as spouses and other intimates—what to cook for dinner, when to take the daughter to ballet, and so on. Thus 2 to 5 percent is left for real communication of self, who we are, what we feel. In organizations the entire 100 percent of our time is spent on logistics. Thus we need to develop a means to allow for that 2 to 5 percent of intimate communication. Autry does that by bringing managers together to talk about self, feelings, and reactions, with discussion of logistics forbidden. This approach is a modern adaptation of the T-group and similar to Peter Senge's (1990) techniques for creating openness.

Autry is building opportunities for people to speak honestly about what they are doing, to break down competition and ego, so they can realize that all people do not have to have the same capabilities. A true community has people with many different abilities and varying motivations. Autry's process seems to be highly effective in removing organizational politics and allowing everyone more space and support to do their jobs well. He agrees with Peter Drucker (1989) that managers must enhance employees' strengths and make their weaknesses irrelevant.

After the three years of transformation work, Autry's efforts have paid off. Not only does the organization in Sydney now have more energy and life, but its profits have tripled since Autry began working with them.

What Makes for Love and
Spirituality in the Workplace?

How to get from here to there is the problem. Many organizations declare certain values but do not act on them. Accomplishing love in the workplace is an issue of operationalizing the concepts and ideas that many organizations have embraced as important and even vital to successful and vigorous organizations.

Chris Argyris (1993) calls this the difference between espoused theories and theories in action. Kerr (1995) calls it the folly of rewarding A while hoping for B. A recent study found that Kerr's folly is still widespread in more than half the companies polled (Dechant and Veiga, 1995). Managers reported that while they hope for teamwork, they reward the best team members; they hope for innovation and risk taking but reward proven "no mistake" methods; and they hope for employee empowerment and involvement but reward heavy controls over resources and operations.

How does your organization do with putting its theories into practice? One way to find out is to examine what kinds of employees, culture, and workplace atmosphere you desire, and what you are doing to achieve those goals. Are your behaviors productive to those ends, or are you merely rewarding A while hoping for B? Exhibit 5.1 presents some examples of behaviors that companies actually reward, behaviors they hope for, and what needs to be changed for the company to get what it hopes for. The exhibit also contains some blank spaces for you to fill in.

Changing Patterns

How to break out of these unproductive and even dysfunctional patterns of being far away from acting on espoused theories? The first requirement is a commitment to long-term organizational health. Without this long view, managers will be too easily pulled by quarterly profits and the statements on the annual report. This commitment includes a willingness on the part of management to do the following:

Exhibit 5.1. Actual Behavior Versus Hoped-For Behavior.

What we reward	What we are hoping for	What we need to change to get what we hope for
1. Political man-euvering and positioning of self	Quality work and authenticity of behaviors	Communication: openness, dialogue, and transparency (trustworthiness, unity, respect)
2. Not straying too far away from the CEO's ideas	Innovation and creativity	Environment: to be more forgiving and accepting of mistakes (respect, trust-worthiness)
3. Efficiency: handle customers as fast as possible	Service	Balance: between efficiency and caring (justice, service, love)
4.		
5.		
6.		
7.		

1. Work to increase trust from below and, in the words of Autry (1991), trust beyond reason.

2. Open the lines of communication: be accessible, remove hierarchical barriers that intimidate employees, manage by walking around, and finally, listen with respect.

3. Let go of some control, and practice this often. Your employees likely will have some good ideas to act on.

Once these commitments have been made, the next step is to organize a means of communicating and sharing ideas and creating a shared vision. To achieve this, I recommend using one of three technologies—consultation (described in detail in Chapter Four), dialogue, or future search. Each of these methods works in a slightly different manner and for somewhat different purposes. But each of them is based on the New Management Virtues of unity, trustworthiness, respect, and justice.

Consultation is solution driven and requires purity of motive from each participant, as well as frank and respectful exchanges, in order for the "spark of truth" to come from the "clash of differing opinions" (Rabbani, 1968, p. 21). Dialogue is less structured, but requires each person to speak, usually as long as is needed, without interruption. Its purpose is to find common ground and shifting paradigms. The goal of future search is to bring various stakeholders together to create an agenda to solve thorny issues or create new strategies. The time requirements are different for each strategy. Consultation can be done in long or short time frames, while dialogue works best with large blocks of time, measured in days. To do what future search is designed for, three full days are needed. Exhibit 5.2 summarizes these and additional features of the three strategies.

What is needed is an initial coming together of people from all levels of the organization, as well as some outside stakeholders, to honestly assess where the organization is. How do its mission, culture, values, and practices stand up to scrutiny using a spiritually based framework? These sessions will be nearly worthless unless they are frank and forthright (while respectful) and unless there is a basis for action afterward. Otherwise, management will create cynicism and greater suspicion than before. Employees rarely get asked by management if they are treated with respect, if justice pervades the environment, whether there is unity, and most important, if there is trust toward and from higher levels.

If consultation or dialogue is chosen, possible questions with which to start might include the following:

When have you been trusted or mistrusted in this organization? How have you experienced a loss of trustworthiness?

Share a significant experience in which you were treated with respect or disrespect and tell how it influenced your attitudes and behavior.

Exhibit 5.2. Three Group Technologies for Sharing Ideas and Creating a Shared Vision.

	Consultation	Dialogue	Future Search
Purpose	Seeks truth; is solution driven; moves toward unity.	Achieves sense of community; finds common ground; moves toward making a paradigm shift.	Seeks common ground and builds community in order to develop a long-range plan to overcome problems or bring about cultural change.
Boundaries	Members must be committed to finding best solution.	Takes potentially more time than consultation, but less than future search.	Takes three days to do adequately.
Main features	Participants speak own views and feelings with respect—from clash of differing opinions comes the spark of truth.	Each participant speaks own truth without interruption— may use talking ball or stick. Has minimum structure.	Representatives of all stakeholder groups meet and are given tasks according to well-defined agenda and format; subgroups leave with specific tasks to accomplish.

Have you been part of a situation that either created or destroyed unity?

When did someone act toward you with justice or injustice and what was the effect on you?

What has been your experience with service and humility in this company?

These questions need to be considered on a personal level rather than as abstract ideas. It is important for the facilitator to gently keep the group on that track. Ideally, the group would ultimately police itself. When groups veer off into impersonal discussion, the connection of group members to one another and the power to create unity are lost.

Another task for the group could be to discuss the following list of organizational goals and changes to see how relevant and workable they might be. Many of the changes recommended are appearing more frequently in various management publications (Pfeffer, 1995). The virtues needed for each change are shown in parentheses.

1. Recruit the best employees who share common values and a common work ethic (unity).

2. Make sure the company mission helps people to feel that what they are doing has meaning and importance (respect).

3. Let people do what they do best (trustworthiness).

4. Invest in their training and development, both for the betterment of their work and to send a message that they are worthy partners, as well as to make them more employable in case of business downturns (trustworthiness, respect, justice).

5. Reward employees fairly and with incentives so they can see that their contributions are valued and appreciated, but avoid pay schemes that splinter work groups (justice, unity).

6. Give employees a piece of the action or some sense of financial ownership of the company, again increasing incentives and the sense of partnership (justice).

7. Share all information all the time. In fact, flood the organization with data, letting employees learn to sort through it. This often requires extra training for employees in reading balance sheets and so on, but it is well worth the effort. Secrets rarely remain that way and have a way of increasing cynicism once leaked (trustworthiness, respect).

8. Use collaborative decision making, participation, and empowerment. These methods require letting go on the part of top management and a willingness for people at the lower levels to take risks. Make that sure employees know their opinions count (respect, unity, trustworthiness).

9. Remove the extremes of the hierarchical system, whether the symbolic perquisites such as parking lots, dining rooms, and executive suites, or the more economic perquisites of huge CEO salaries, especially in times of financial belt-tightening for everyone else (justice).

10. Be customer oriented. Create systems that respond to the customer, hire people sensitive to customer needs, help them to understand the needs of customers more clearly and train them to better meet those needs, and reward them for doing so. To achieve this, the organization also needs to have a sense of service to the employees. Employees who feel respected and have a sense of job security generally have more of a commitment to customers (service, respect).

11. Be a "family friendly" company (respect).

12. Inspire, inspire, inspire with vision (unity).

This in-depth discussion must be followed up regularly with other sessions of consultation or dialogue in order to ensure the

**Exhibit 5.3. How Is My Company Achieving
the New Management Virtues?**

New Management Virtue	Current situation and practices: to what extent are they following each virtue?	What do we need to do to work toward this virtue?
Trustworthiness		
Unity		
Respect and Dignity		
Justice		
Service and Humility		

integrity of the programs, that is, that the operationalization of the company's theories is loyal to spiritual law or the New Management Virtues. The worksheet provided in Exhibit 5.3 can be used to examine this correspondence.

Exhibit 5.4 contains another list of questions that may be used in this meeting as well as in daily management practice. These questions have helped me a great deal when I am trying to decide what to do. Recently I was in a situation where a colleague treated me unjustly. According to certain models I would have been justified in being assertive and critical. As a result of the following list, however, I was forced to ask whether those behaviors would create unity; the answer was no and I had to revise my strategy. Instead, I talked to the colleague, listening to her point of view in order to understand why she had acted as she had. Just the simple act of really listening to her changed my perceptions and influenced how I explained my reactions and feelings. We ended up with positive feelings rather than the resentments that would have been expected had I insisted only on justice.

Exhibit 5.4. Is It Spiritual?

Questions to Ask	Situation 1/ Proposed Behavior	Situation 2/ Proposed Behavior	Situation 3/ Proposed Behavior
Programs, HR Policies, or Behaviors of Managers			
1. Is it trustworthy? (Is it honest and transparent?)			
2. Does it create unity?			
3. Does it maintain dignity?			
4. Are my intentions pure? Am I detached?			
5. Is it just?			
6. Is it done in a spirit of service?			
7. Does it show humility?			
8. Would I be ashamed if others knew about it?			
9. Does it demonstrate and develop competence?			
10. Would I want to be treated this way? Would the other person(s) want me to behave this way (Wisdom of Love)?			

If It Looks Like One, It Is

What do love and spirituality look like in an organization? How are they manifested and what encourages or discourages their development? If we had some idea of these issues, we could work toward the goal of having the roots of organizational love and spirituality.

Exhibit 5.5 illustrates how the desire to become a better person and strive for higher goals helps the individual's spiritual growth, while obsession with self, material possessions, or status hampers such growth. In groups, spirituality is manifested in acceptance of diversity, searching for many solutions, and valuing each person's contribution; it is blocked by power trips, political games, and double standards for different status levels. When teams are spiritual they are more accepting of diversity and nurturing of dissimilar ideas and views. Spirituality in organizations would show itself as equitable and just distribution of resources, including removal of most management perks, eliminating abuses of power or privilege, empowering employees by treating them respectfully as adults, and seeing workers as human souls rather than as human resources. Impediments come in the form of manipulations to gain power, dishonesty of management, and a greater concern for profits than for people.

The New Management Virtues at Work

Through trial and error, companies worldwide are discovering the effectiveness the New Management Virtues of unity, respect, justice, trustworthiness, and service. The results can be quite impressive.

Bell Labs, where I consulted for a number of years, has "hot groups" whose members act like they are in love—in love, that is, with the task and the work (Leavitt and Lipman-Blumen, 1995). They have boundless energy and take on extra work with gusto, engage in spirited sharing and clashing of ideas, and are passionate about what they are doing. How does an organization encourage such task obsession? Not by driving and controlling. An emphasis on people nourishes the "hot groups that focus tirelessly on tasks" (p. 113). What that means to me is that when organizations work toward increasing spirituality and the New Management Virtues, they can help to bring about the kinds of motivation most companies only dream about.

Amoco Corporation has embarked on a major change effort, parts of which embody many of the New Management Virtues, with a move toward, by my definition, a more spiritual base. The company's goals include to "respect the individual rights and dignity of all people" and show "honesty, fair and trustworthy behavior in all our activities" (Buckles, 1996). In order to operationalize their espoused values, they developed progress principles, initiatives, and practices, which listed specific desired behaviors. Since

Exhibit 5.5. Love and Spirituality at Different Organizational Levels.

	What Does Love and Spirituality Look Like?	What Helps Develop Love and Spirituality?	What Blocks Love and Spirituality?	What Are Loving and Spiritual Outcomes?
Individual	Person becomes more honest, fair, and dignified, and strives for competence and excellence.	Desire to become a better person, to strive for higher goals, to serve others.	Narcissism; obsession with status; focus on the "seen" acquisition of material goods, status; focus on the "seen" world.	Steadfast focus on developing New Management Virtues and serving others.
Team	Groups more accepting of diverse styles and members; real listening takes place; members willing to detach from own ideas and agendas and search for "best" solutions.	Groups welcome new members, practice inquiry skills, seek diversity, encourage frank and loving communication.	Power and political games, rigid behavior norms, seek Groupthink; member value based on status; double standard for high- and low-status members.	Organic unity of members, who nonetheless maintain individuality.

Organization			
Equitable and fair distribution of resources; removal of most "perks" for management; willingness to see people with individual needs rather than as human resources; open/fair/respectful communication up-down and down-up.	Hierarchy is flattened; removal of position-privilege; workers truly empowered; managers are coaches not cops; employees trusted and treated as adults; higher levels do not abuse power or take advantage of authority.	Lack of trustworthiness and honesty by managers; higher levels preserve maximum power; managers manipulate to gain goals; organization more concerned with profits than with people.	Capacity development of all members; high energy and commitment levels; sharing and connectedness; a real community.
Society			
Change in institutions of society to reflect extreme reduction of prejudice and privilege; rewards based more on meritocracy; move away from power-based to truth-seeking institutions.	True justice in legal system; equal access to education; acceptance of various cultural and ethnic groups; lack of oppressive policies toward any ethnic or class groups or women.	Legal and political power tightly held in the hands of a corrupt elite; repression and abuse of lower classes and certain other groups; dishonesty and corruption seen as necessities for survival.	Development of potential of all groups of society; unity of various regions and groups; organic wholeness of society.

Source: Adapted from Watkins and Marsick, 1993, p. 263.

beginning this program in 1988, Amoco's financial situation has greatly improved. Return on equity has increased, stock price has improved by about 34 percent in five years, and net profit went up 25 percent from 1994 to 1995.

Idea Connection Systems has worked hard to explicitly operationalize spirituality in its work practices. President Robert Rosenfeld (1996) catalyzed resources in the company to define the various stakeholders and identify what spiritually based behaviors would be, as well naming the dark sides of those qualities. Backbiting, for example, has serious and deleterious effects on a group, for it is not only extremely divisive (creating disunity) but it also quenches the soul of the individual and the group. Idea Connection Systems has an explicit rule against backbiting. Rosenfeld told me that it "demoralizes the other person; it lowers the station of the other person in your eyes. It's not healthy" (personal communication, August 1996). Rosenfeld works hard to infuse each person with the company value that they should assume purity of motive on the part of others. In fact, this attitude is part of the written codes of the company.

Delta Airlines was able to reduce erosion of trust during a major restructuring by increasing both the quality and the quantity of communications (Richardson and Denton, 1996). The company set up a special 800 number to handle questions from employees and to give information updates on the changes. The 800 line received more than six thousand calls a day in the beginning. A similar program was done at another company going through a merger, and within three months of the announcement, trust and job satisfaction had actually increased.

A word of caution on increasing communication: though the cutting-edge folk wisdom is to flood the organization with information and to communicate more, how—and what—you communicate are important considerations, too. It has always been surprising to me how many managers think they can fool employees by denying rumors that are actually true or by pretending to listen to ideas they have no intention of implementing. People can see through these devices, and they end up more cynical than ever. Reduced trust is also inevitable when values are espoused but not lived. When the expectation is broken that values are best communicated through actions, employees punish the company and turn around slogans; for example, "Quality is everything we make" becomes "Quality is everything we fake"; "Beliefs We Share" becomes "[expletive] We Share"; and "Working with Pride" becomes "Working for [expletive]" (Larkin and Larkin, 1996).

Face-to-face communication is far superior to videotaped announcements or newsletters. The personal approach, when done sincerely and honestly with no game playing, can increase trust and unity. A danger of technology is the ease with which meetings can be conducted in cyberspace. The emotional and spiritual bonds of relationships are best built through in-person interactions, because as Tom Peters says, "You can pretend to care. You can't pretend to be there" (1996, p. 148). Without these emotional and spiritual bonds, managers have no chance to build up an "emotional bank account" that can be drawn on during times of conflict or stress (Covey, 1989).

Developing an environment in which there is respect, unity, justice, and service requires good people skills for all employees, not just managers. When Coca-Cola trained the 104 employees at its Baltimore syrup plant in listening, conflict management, group dynamics, and team problem solving, it was able to change from a seniority-based to a performance-based system, and it was able to increase production by 16 percent and productivity by 7 percent (Phillips, 1996).

To increase customer satisfaction to 100 percent, guaranteed, Hampton Inns implemented empowerment through respecting and trusting employees, giving them authority to act on customer needs, including the ability to grant a free overnight stay (Sowder, 1996). As a result of this new program, employee turnover decreased 20 percent, while revenues increased dramatically, by an estimated $12 million.

Conclusion

These success stories are fundamentally about hope. With all the negative stories around, it would be easy to say that organizations are so unspiritual that we might as well give up any attempt to develop in that direction. That love is so indiscernible and nearly impossible to achieve it seems hopeless to try. Or that virtues are so rare and difficult to maintain in the current business environment, what's the point of trying? The experiences of these leading companies demonstrate that such hopelessness is unwarranted.

Even where positive results are yet to be recorded, we should not despair. Another way to look at the situation is to see spirituality as a process of growth for organizations, just as it is for individuals. No matter at what point the organization is, it can always move forward. Even as people backslide, so will organizations. We should accept organizations where they are and assist in whatever ways we can in their development, and we should see their growth as a constant striving or even as a type of "continuous improvement."

Love and virtue carry their own rewards, according to spiritual law. You can become more spiritual by following a spiritual path, but you cannot *use* spirituality for your own gain. Instead, love, spiritual law, and virtue can help you to see the essential nobility of yourself and others and apply this nobility to the world of business. In doing so, you can understand the beauty and meaning of those things that are invisible and intangible, yet all-pervasive and indispensable. This is the Wisdom of Love.

> *The invincible weapon, always victorious, is the incessant act of love.*
>
> —Sister Consalata, seventeenth century

> *The salvation of the world lies in the human heart.*
>
> —Vaclav Havel, 1985

Addendum

Because this book is about spiritual development and growth, I think it is important to share my personal experience with this. I grew up as a Christian, a Lutheran, and was very active in Luther League as a youth in Wisconsin. My childhood was less than ideal, and my anchor has been my love of God. Even at seven years old I would go to church alone, the only one in my family who seemed interested in it at the time.

When I went to college I expanded my spiritual search beyond the Lutheran Church and began what I see now as my real journey of healing, both emotionally and spiritually. For nearly four years I visited churches, temples, synagogues, and anything I could find that might promise a spark of truth. There were some sparks, some love, in a number of the places I visited and in the works I read, but mostly not enough to satisfy me.

I eventually stumbled across the Baha'i Faith, but it took me many months to realize it was what I was looking for. Initially, I discounted it as anything serious, for by this time I was quite worn out with organized religion, which I saw as irrelevant and oppressive to believers. At the same time I was also studying dance of India and my teacher suggested I read Swami Vivekannanda. I went to the library and devoured several books of his, and also found some by Martin Luther King Jr. Reading these books caused a spiritual awakening within me. Here were two men who seemed to me to be highly spiritual and highly religious. Each had made a difference in the world through faith and belief in God and through their religion. Only then did I realize that religion did not have to be irrelevant nor oppressive. Only then did I seriously listen to what the Baha'is were saying and realize I had found the object of my quest.

As a result of this awareness, I spent the next twenty-five years learning about my own spirituality and about what fosters spiritual growth. My search has led me to the scriptures and teachings of Buddhism, Hinduism, Islam, Confucianism, Judaism, Christianity, Zoroastrianism, and Baha'i, in which I have found amazing similarities as well as relevance for today's managers.

Endnotes

Preface

1. Love can be of different types. C. S. Lewis (1960) talks about natural Need-love versus the selfless Gift-love, which he calls Charity. Romantic love, or Eros, is differentiated from Charity by Lewis, and this book will focus on Charity, leaving Eros in the workplace for others to discuss.

Prelude

1. An example may help to illustrate our relationship to this other world. When I was in college and in the early years of my spiritual journey, one of my favorite books was *Flatland*, a book written in the 1980s by British mathematician Edwin Abbott. *Flatland* took place in a two-dimensional world where people were either low-status triangles or higher-status polygons. They saw each other as lines, though, since it was the two-dimensional side of a triangle looking at the two-dimensional side of a polygon. Houses and buildings were merely lines with open spaces for doors. However, to the two-dimensional people, these lines appeared to be walls. Every thousand years, a sphere would pass through Flatland to preach the gospel of the Three-Dimensional World. It would look like a dot, then a small circle that kept enlarging and finally shrinking and disappearing. The three-dimensional sphere could look down and see everything in Flatland, including the inside of houses and people. As it passed through Flatland, the polygon it had chosen would be

very confused by the "circle," which kept changing size, then disappearing, while continuing to talk. In fact, the sphere would merely be a slight distance up from Flatland, talking down at the polygon. We live in a kind of Flatland. It is a three-dimensional Flatland, but we can imagine another dimension in addition to what we see before us. The world of spirit is the other dimension, which is invisible to us but existent nonetheless. In the world of spirit, we can see things that are not obvious from the perspective of the material world.

2. An excellent reference for this is H.T.D. Rost's *The Golden Rule*, published in Oxford, England, by George Ronald Press, 1986.

3. Many of the quotations from Zoroastrianism are taken from either *Sacred Books of the East*, volume 31 (*The Zendavesta*), or Farhang Mehr's *The Zoroastrian Tradition* (1991). The three wise men who searched for the Bethlehem star are believed to have been Zoroastrians. "Magi" is the anglicized version of the Persian word "mogh," which means Zoroastrian priest. And according to the *Bible Dictionary* (Novotny, 1956, p. 452), the magi referred to in both Daniel 2:2 and Matthew 2:1 were Zoroastrian priests, and possibly astronomers or astrologers as well. Finally, Mehr (1991) confirms the Magi were the clerics of Zoroastrianism.

4. Dates obtained from religious scholars Susan Maneck, Vahid Behmardi, and Moojan Momen, as well as *The New Grolier Multimedia Encyclopedia* (1992). Some Hindu quotes are from Momen (1990).

5. According to Maneck, Behmardi, and Momen there are differing opinions on the beginning of Zoroastrianism. The best current estimates are based on the hypothesis that Zoroaster, the founder, lived sometime between 1000 and 1500 B.C.

6. There is a difference in regional practices of religion that may be explained by Hofstede's four cultural dimensions, particularly masculinity and femininity (1991, p. 102). Masculine cultures tend to value achievement, material possessions, competition,

worldly success, and decisive managers, while feminine cultures (not to be confused with feminism) value community, relationships, family, tenderness, cooperation, and consensus-seeking managers. Masculine countries, such as the United States, are more likely to value the "emotional meaning of God's name," rather than the importance of following any religious commandments or changing to more virtuous behavior.

7. What effect does love have on the loved one? According to a study using four hundred case examples of admired leaders, these leaders caused people to feel "valued, motivated, enthusiastic, challenged, inspired, capable, supported, powerful, and respected" (Kouzes and Posner, 1993, p. 30) In all four hundred cases the leader caused upliftment of spirit and enhanced self-concept. Kouzes and Posner further argue that when subordinates have *love* or *affection* for the leader, the subordinates will work harder and more effectively.

8. Quoted in Canfield and Hansen, 1993, p. 1.

Chapter One

1. While we long for unconditional love, we rarely give it out (Hormann, 1994). Instead, our love often has demands, requirements, and expectations of paybacks, as though we have a little calculator going off inside our brain to determine what levels and types of in-kind obligations are expected.

2. It is one of the paradoxes of life (including organizational life) that by going directly after something we oftentimes do not get it. By trying to get people to respect me or love me or care for me, I often push them away. Yet if I respect them, love them, and show care, I will experience their love. It is only by being selfless rather than self-centered that we get what we are after. That is why the "pursuit of happiness" is an elusive dream. True happiness is a by-product of loving others, doing something well, or being part of a higher purpose. That is the meaning of the Christian scripture, "For whosoever will save his life shall

lose it; and whosoever will lose his life for my sake shall find it" (Matthew 16:25).

3. The best behavior is to do the right thing for the right reason, for pure motive. However, it is better to do the right thing for the wrong reason (expectation of rewards) than to do the wrong thing.

Chapter Two

1. In recent times we have witnessed traumatic restructuring resulting in hundreds of thousands of job casualties. We have seen big-time corporate espionage charges. For example, General Motors claimed that Volkswagen stole vital secrets through their then-new (and now fired) executive, GM's former J. Ignacio Lopez de Arriortua. Similarly, American Airlines accused Northwest Airlines of stealing vital computer and mathematical information on passenger scheduling, the knowledge of which had given American an edge of $300 million per year in revenues. Other major problems have been exorbitant salaries paid to CEOs, often at the same time as major staff or salary cuts for everyone else. Alienated workers abound. They are disenfranchised by the wrenching restructurings, or they are the "working dead," cut off from any meaningful work or contribution, or they are abused by their systems for so long they become, as one stated, "just your average worker who quits emotionally but shows up for the paycheck."

2. "Managing *only* for profit is like playing tennis with your eye on the scoreboard and not on the ball" (Blanchard and Peale, 1988, p. 106).

Chapter Three

1. One notable exception to this refrain is Miloslav Handl (1994), CEO of SETUZA in the Czech Republic, who said, "We tried

so many things in order for our company to be successful. But what worked best was becoming more trustworthy."

2. The prayer often used in the recovery movement is relevant here: "God, grant me the serenity to accept the things I cannot change, the courage to change the things I can, and the wisdom to know the difference." Ernie Kurtz, historian of Alcoholics Anonymous, has this to say about the authorship of what has come to be known as the Serenity Prayer: "As for the Serenity Prayer, most commonly attribute it to Reinhold Niebuhr, and that includes his biographer Richard Wrightman Fox as well as several AA members who researched it. I still have doubts: the core idea can be found in Greek stoicism (though not in the prayer format), and there is anecdotal evidence that Niebuhr disclaimed authorship when it was first attributed. Still, the majority opinion does credit it to him. . . . AA adopted the prayer after a member found it in an obituary column in, I believe, the old *New York Herald-Tribune*. In that printing, a clipping of which is in the AA archives, the prayer itself is preceded by the word Mother" (personal communication, 1995).

3. Quoted in Popov (1992).

4. Robert Rosenfeld of Idea Connection Systems (ICS) shared this formula with me. Neither one of us could locate its origins, however.

5. More recently, Iacocca has not fared as well with Chrysler (Glassman, 1995), once again showing the unpredictable future of spirituality in any one company.

6. If we want high-performance companies, we should involve more people through self-managed teams while ensuring that managers listen to experiences and problems and learn to recognize the victories of employees (Peters, 1987). Nearly half of the ten characteristics shown by Nadler and Gerstein (1992) to be vital to creating high-powered work systems relate to empowerment and enriched jobs, both of which are based on respect and dignity. Numerous writers have argued that people

want more challenge, achievement, responsibility, and sense of mission (Drucker, 1993, 1996).

Employee involvement may take many forms. One form that has been around longer than the new management paradigm is Herzberg's (1968) *job enrichment,* in which vertical loading of jobs (adding higher level, management-type tasks to the job) allows workers to make some or all of their own supervisory decisions. The modern term for this concept is *empowerment.*

7. Leo Montada of Germany's Center for Empirical Justice Research has conducted numerous studies on justice and has found that even in varied cultures people have a fundamental sense of justice. We react both to being treated unfairly and with a bad conscience from seeing others suffer injustices. Sometimes this gets played out with the "advantaged" closing their eyes to great disparities or with the privileged giving large amounts of money to assuage their consciences. Montada said that justice is an anthropological constant, and that the "justice motive" is present in every social system (personal communication, April 1995).

8. MIT economist Martin Weitzman has the idea of making pay "float" to reflect company performance, which would create a "share economy" (Kanter, 1990). The advantages of this approach would be not only that it would produce higher motivation to do quality work, but also that it would help organizations survive during business slumps and would even encourage companies to hire extra workers, because they would be paid only in proportion to what they would bring in. The virtue of justice would be working for both employees and executives/owners. Many more companies are realizing the benefits of paying for performance and using bonuses to do so. Two studies of labor contracts show increases from 1984 to 1986 in the use of bonuses, from about 6 percent of contracts to 20 percent (Kanter, 1987).

9. There are a number of ways to do this. One is to design and implement a corporate strategy in which the main focus is on continually increasing the value to customers and that includes many evolving techniques in which service, quality, and customer satisfaction together produce perceived and real customer value (Band, 1991). Many books and articles have come out in recent years that go into useful detail on how one goes about improving the service component and orientation of a business.

Chapter Four

1. A few years ago I was doing some consulting and research in the area of organizational innovation and had the occasion to talk to some directors of innovation around the United States. One spoke with regret in his voice, describing how the company's fixation on team playing had hurt his department, which was part of research and development. Five years previously the company had decided to run its divisions with teams. The idea probably came from the management workshops and books that managers had read, the director told me. They fired everyone who wasn't a "team player." It took several years to realize that those loners, those weirdos, were the ones coming up with all the new ideas. "Now we are innovation poor," he lamented. What they discovered, too late, was that having diversity of people can create an incubator for new ideas and novel approaches, particularly if the group can harness those differences in an effective manner.

2. Ben & Jerry's has been accused of unfair business practices by one of its suppliers of chocolate chip cookies. In addition, there was some question as to whether their "rain forest" nuts were legitimate. They have since changed the rain forest label. Here is another example of how no company, and perhaps no human system, can be perfectly spiritual.

References

Aaron, H. (1994, February 10). The myth of the heartless businessman. *The Wall Street Journal Europe*, p. 10.

Abbott, E. (1926). *Flatland: A romance of many dimensions* (3rd ed.). New York: Oxford University Press.

'Abdu'l-Bahá. (1969). *Paris talks*. London: Baha'i Publishing Trust.

Adams, J. D. (Ed.). (1984a). *Transforming work*. Alexandria, VA: Miles River Press.

Adams, J. D. (1984b). Achieving and maintaining personal peak performance. In J. D. Adams (Ed.), *Transforming work* (pp. 139–53). Alexandria, VA: Miles River Press.

Alburty, S. (1997, January). The ad agency to end all ad agencies. *Fast Company*, pp. 116–124.

Al-Quran: A contemporary translation by Ahmed Ali. (1988). Princeton: Princeton University Press.

Argyris, C. (1993). *Knowledge for action: A guide for overcoming barriers to organizational change.* San Francisco: Jossey-Bass.

Argyris, C., & Schön, D. A. (1974). *Theory in practice: Increasing professional effectiveness.* San Francisco: Jossey-Bass.

Autry, J. A. (1991). *Love and profit.* New York: Morrow.

Badii, H. (1993). *The true foundation of all economics.* St. Vincent, West Indies: Author.

Bahá'u'lláh. (1990). *The Hidden Words.* Wilmette, IL: Baha'i Publishing Trust. (Original work published 1932)

Bahá'u'lláh. (1976). *Gleanings from the writings of Bahá'u'lláh.* Wilmette, IL: Baha'i Publishing Trust.

Bahá'u'lláh. (1978). *Tablets of Bahá'u'lláh.* Haifa, Israel: Baha'i World Centre.

Band, W. A. (1991). *Creating value for customers: Designing and implementing a total corporate strategy.* New York: Wiley.

Bartholomé, F., & Laurent, A. (1986). The manager: Master and servant of power. *Harvard Business Review, 64*(6), 77–81.

The Bhagavad-Gita: The Geeta (Shri Purohit Swami, Trans.). (1986). London: Faber and Faber.

The Bhagavad Gita as it is (Bhaktivedanta Swami Prabhupada, Trans.). (1972). New York: Macmillan.

The Bhagavad Gita (Juan Mascaró, Trans.). (1984). Harmondsworth: Penguin.

The Bhagavad-Gita (R. C. Zachner, Trans.). (1969). Oxford: Clarendon Press.

Bird, L. (1996, June 12). High-tech inventory system coordinates retailer's clothes with customers' taste. *The Wall Street Journal*, p. B1.

Blanchard, K., & Peale, N. V. (1988). *The power of ethical management.* New York: Morrow.

Blueprints for success. (1995, August 1). *Printing Impressions*, p. 32.

Bollier, D. (1996). *Aiming higher.* New York: AMACOM.

Branegan, J. (1994, October 31). White knights need not apply. *Time*, pp. 70–73.

Brokaw, L. (1995, December). Like money for chocolate. *Hemispheres*, pp. 5–38.

Buckles, R. J. (1996, Winter). Profiting from customer-driven quality at Amoco Corporation. *National Productivity Review*, pp. 63–78.

Bukhārī, I. (1976). Ṣaḥīḥ al-Bukhārī (Vol. I, Book 2, Number 12). Chicago: Kazi Publications.

Bull, N. J. (1969). *Moral judgment from childhood to adolescence.* New York: Routledge.

Canfield, J., & Hansen, M. V. (1993). *Chicken soup for the soul.* Deerfield Beach, FL: Health Communications.

Cantu, C. (1994). *Unity in diversity.* Annual report. ServiceMaster Corporation.

Chappell, T. (1993). *The soul of a business.* New York: Bantam.

Clark, D. (1996, January 18). Novell tries to drag itself from a not-so-perfect merger. *The Wall Street Journal Europe*, *13*(245), 4.

Collins, J. C., & Porras, J. I. (1994). *Built to last.* New York: HarperCollins.

Confucius. (1992). *Confucius, the Analects* (Lun yu). Philadelphia: Coronet Books.

Cookson Group. (1996, September 5). *Cookson 1996 interim financial results and 1995 financial results.* London: Author.

Covey, S. R. (1989a). *The seven habits of highly effective people.* New York: Simon & Schuster.

Covey, S. R. (1989b, December). Moral compassing. *Executive Excellence*, pp. 7–8.

Czech privitisation: But Custer lost. (1994, June 25). *The Economist*, *331*(7869), 66–67.

The Dhammapada (Irving Babbitt, Trans.). (1965). New York: New Direction.

The Dhammapada (Juan Mascaró, Trans.). (1973). Harmondsworth: Penguin.

Downs, A. (1995, October). The truth about layoffs. *Management Review*, pp. 57–61.

Drucker, P. F. (1989). *The new realities.* New York: HarperCollins.

Drucker, P. F. (1993). *Managing for the future.* New York: NAL/Dutton.

Drucker, P. F. (1996). *The leader of the future.* San Francisco: Jossey-Bass.

Dubashi, J. (1994, Fall). God is my reference point. *Financial World*, pp. 36–37.

Emerson, R. W. (1844). Politics. In *Essays: Second series*.

Evered, R., & Selman, J. (1988) Managers anonymous. *New Management*, 6(2), 56–61.

Farnham, A. (1993, September 20). Mary Kay's lessons in leadership. *Fortune*, pp. 68–77.

Fleet Sheet, 1993.

Flynn, G. (1996). Hallmark cares. *Personnel Journal*, 75(3), 50–61.

Fozdar, J. K. (1973). *The god of Buddha*. New York: Asia Publishing House.

Fraker, A. T., & Spears, L. C. (Eds.). (1996). *Seeker and servant: Reflections on religious leadership*. San Francisco: Jossey-Bass.

Frankl, V. E. (1984). *Man's search for meaning*. New York: Simon & Schuster.

Frick, D. M., & Spears, L. C. (Eds.). (1996). *On becoming a servant leader: The private writings of Robert K. Greenleaf*. San Francisco: Jossey-Bass.

Fukuyama, F. (1995). *Trust: The social virtues and the creation of prosperity*. New York: Free Press.

Galbraith, J. R., Lawler, E. E. III, & Associates (1993). *Organizing for the future: The new logic for managing complex organizations*. San Francisco: Jossey-Bass.

Glassman, J. (1995, July 19). Did you buy a new car from this man? *The Wall Street Journal*, p. A8.

Glatzer, N. H. (Ed. and Trans.). (1969). *The Judaic tradition*. Boston: Beacon.

Green, F. B., & Hatch, E. (1990). Involvement and commitment in the workplace: A new ethic evolving. *Advanced Management Journal*, 55(4), 8–12.

Greenleaf, R. K. (1977). *Servant leadership*. New York: Paulist Press.

Greig, R. (1996, June 1). Pure gold: 1996 National Association of Printers and Lithographers Management Plus Competition Awards. *American Printer*, p. 42.

Hagemann, H. (1994, October 27). Promoting profits through part-time work. *The Wall Street Journal Europe*, 12(190), 10.

Hammer, M., & Champy, J. (1993). *Reengineering the corporation: A manifesto for business revolution*. New York: HarperCollins.

Handl, M. (1994, December). *Vnitrni a vnejsi etika akciove spolecnosti* [Ethics inside and outside the business community]. Presentation at the Business and Ethics Conference, Prague.

Hardaker, M., & Ward, B. K. (1991). How to make a team work. *Harvard Business Review*, 65(6), 112–120.

Harley, W. B. (1995, Autumn). A general purpose consensus problem-solving model. *Team Performance Management*.

Harman, W. W., & Hormann, J. (1990). *Creative work*. Indianapolis: Knowledge Systems.

Havel, V. (1985). *Living in truth*. London: Faber and Faber.

Hawley, J. (1993). *Reawakening the spirit in work*. San Francisco: Berrett-Koehler.

Hayek, F. A. (1948). *Individualism and economic order*. Chicago: University of Chicago Press.

Heider, J. (1985). *The Tao of leadership*. New York: Bantam.

Henkoff, R. (1992, June 29). Piety, profits and productivity. *Fortune*, pp. 84–85.

Herman, S. (1994). Building company spirit in multidimensional organizations. Unpublished doctoral dissertation, University of Massachusetts, Amherst.

Herzberg, F. (1987). One more time: How do you motivate employees? *Harvard Business Review, 65*(5), 109–120.

Hewlett-Packard. (1989). *The HP way*. Palo Alto, CA: Author.

Hofstede, G. (1991). *Cultures and organizations*. London: McGraw-Hill.

The Holy Bible (Revised English Version). (1989). Oxford: Oxford University Press.

Hormann, J. (1994). Glaube und liebe. Unpublished manuscript.

The I ching or book of changes (3d ed.). (1967). Richard Wilhelm's translation rendered into English by Cary F. Baynes. Princeton, N.J.: Princeton University Press.

Jackall, R. (1988). *Moral mazes*. New York: Oxford University Press.

Jenkins, H. W. Jr. (1996, December 11). VW and GM should stop complaining. *The Wall Street Journal Europe, 14*(221), 6.

Kanter, R. M. (1987). The attack on pay. *Harvard Business Review, 65*(2), 60–67.

Katha Upanishad, Taittiriya Upanishad, Mundaka Upanishad (Swami Sharvananda, Trans.). (1949–1950). Madras: Sri Ramakrisna.

Kerr, S. (1995). An academy classic: On the folly of rewarding A, while hoping for B. *Academy of Management Executive, 9*(1), 7–16.

King, N. Jr. (1994, May 25). Tatra Board to ponder fate of US managers. *The Wall Street Journal Europe*, p. 3.

Knecht, G. B. (1994, September 8). How a Texas college mortgaged its future in derivatives failure. *The Wall Street Journal Europe, 12*(169), 1, 7.

Koestenbaum, P. (1991). *Leadership: The inner side of greatness*. San Francisco: Jossey-Bass.

Kouzes, J. M., & Posner, B. Z. (1993). *Credibility: How leaders gain and lose it, why people demand it*. San Francisco: Jossey-Bass.

Lao Tsu. (1989). *Tao te ching*. New York: Vintage Books.

Larkin, T. J., & Larkin, S. (1996, May). Reaching and changing frontline employees. *Harvard Business Review*, pp. 95–104.

Lawton, R. (1993). *Creating a customer-centered culture: Leadership in quality innovation*. Milwaukee: Quality Press.

Leavitt, H. J., & Lipman-Blumen, J. (1995, July-August). Hot groups. *Harvard Business Review*, pp. 109–116.

Levering, R., & Moskowitz, M. (1993). *The one hundred best companies to work for in America*. New York: Doubleday.

Lewis, C. S. (1960, 1988). *The four loves*. New York: Harcourt Brace.

Liebig, J. E. (1994). *Merchants of vision*. San Francisco: Berrett-Koehler.

London, J. (1984). *Martin Eden*. New York: Viking Books.

Lopez, J. A. (1993). Undivided attention: How PepsiCo gets work out of people. *The Wall Street Journal Europe, 11*(45), 1, 11.

Lowes, J. (1994, Spring). Long-term plan to benefit TDPartners and customers. *TDNews*, p. 1.

Mack, M. (1992). *L'Emperatif Humain*. Masson, France: Institut de l'Entreprise.

Mahaprajna, Yuvacharya Shri, Shraman Mahavir: His life and teachings. (1980). Houston: Scholarly Public.

Managers differ over basic perceptions of empowerment. (1995, November). *Professional Manager*, p. 18.

Mangelsdorf, M. (1992). The hottest entrepreneurs in America. *Inc., 14*(13), 88–103.

McCormick, D. W. (1994). Spirituality and management. *Journal of Managerial Psychology, 9*(6), 5–8.

Mehr, F. (1991). *The Zoroastrian tradition*. Rockport, MA: Element.

Miller, L. (1991). *Managing quality through teams*. Atlanta, GA: Miller Consulting Group.

Momen, M. (1990). *Hinduism and the Baha'i Faith*. Oxford: George Ronald Press.

Morgan, K. (1953). *Religion of the Hindus*. New York: Ronald Press.

Müeller, F. M. (Ed.). (1981). *The sacred books of the East* (Vol. 31: The Zend-Avesta, Part III: The Yasna, Visparad, Āfrīnagān, Gāhs and mis fragments) (L. H. Mills, Trans.).

Müller, F. M. (Ed.). (1882). *The sacred books of the East* (Vol. 18: Pahlavi texts. Part II: Dadistan-I-Dinik and the epistles of Manuskihar) (E. W. West, Trans.).

Mumford, E., and Hendricks, R. (1996). Business process re-engineering RIP. *People Management, 2*(9), 22–29.

Murray, M. (1995, May 8). Amid record profits, companies continue to lay off employees. *The Wall Street Journal Europe, 13*(67), 1, 5.

Nadler, D. A., & Gerstein, M. S. (1992). Designing high performance work systems: Organizing people, work, technology, and information. In D. A. Nadler, M. S. Gerstein, R. B. Shaw, & Associates, *Organizational architecture* (pp. 110–132). San Francisco: Jossey-Bass.

Nelson, D. (1994). Remarks made at the Baha'i Family Reunion conference, Florida.

New energy saving system pays off for East Texas Baptist University. (1993, Summer). *TDNews*, p. 1.

Novotny, A. (1956). *Biblicky slovník* [Bible dictionary] (R. Boháček, Trans.). Prague: Kalich.

Österberg, R. (1993). *Corporate renaissance*. Mill Valley, CA: Nataraj.

Peck, M. S. (1993). *A world waiting to be born*. New York: Bantam Books.

Peters, T. (1987). *Thriving on chaos*. New York: Knopf.

Peters, T. (1992). *Liberation management*. New York: Knopf.

Peters, T. (1996, June 3). All you need to know. *Forbes ASAP*, pp. 146, 148.

Pfeffer, J. (1995, February). Producing sustainable competitive advantage through the effective management of people. *Academy of Management Executive*, 9(1), 55–69.

Phillips, S. N. (1996, January). Teamtraining puts fizz in Cola plant's future. *Personnel Journal*, pp. 87–92.

Pollard, C. W. (1994, May). *Ethics*. Presentation given at a meeting of the Human Resource Management Association of Chicago.

Popov, L. K., Popov, D., and Kavelin, J. (1993). *The virtues guide*. Soft Spring Island, British Columbia: Virtues Project.

The Qur'an. (J. M. Rodwell, Trans.) (2nd rev. and amended ed.). (1876). London: Quaritch.

The Qur'an. (Ahmed Ali, Trans.). (1988). Princeton: Princeton University Press.

Ray, M. L. (1992). The emerging new paradigm in business. In J. Renesch (Ed.), *New traditions in business*. San Francisco: Berrett-Koehler.

Reichheld, F. F. (1996). *The loyalty effect*. Boston: Harvard Business School Press.

Richardson, P., & Denton, D. K. (1996, Summer). Communicating change. *Human Resource Management*, 35(2), 203–216.

Richter, S.-G. (1994, June 7). The benefits of employee ownership. *The Wall Street Journal Europe*, p. 6.

Rosenfeld, R. (1996). *Idea Connection Systems corporate philosophy*. Internal document. Idea Connection Systems.

Rosenfeld, R., & Winger-Bearskin, M. (1991). Innovation through groups: The process of consultation. Unpublished manuscript.

Rost, H.T.D. (1986). *The Golden Rule: A universal ethic*. Oxford, England: George Ronald Press.

Rumi, J. (1988). *This longing*. Putney, VT: Threshold Books.

Schmidt, W. H., & Finnigan, J. P. (1992). *The race without a finish line*. San Francisco: Jossey-Bass.

Schweitzer, A. (1958). *Peace or atomic war*. London: A & C Black.

Scott, M. (1995). Howard Schultz interview. *Business Ethics*, 9(6), 26–29.

Seldes, G. (1985). *The great thoughts*. New York: Ballantine.

Semler, R. (1991). Managing without managers. *Harvard Business Review*, 67(5), 76–84.

Semler, R. (1993). *Maverick*. New York: Warner Books.

Semler, R. (1994). Why my former employees still work for me. *Harvard Business Review*, 72(1), 64–74.

Senge, P. (1990). *The fifth discipline*. New York: Doubleday.

ServiceMaster. (1994). Annual report to the shareholders for 1993. Downer's Grove, IL: ServiceMaster Corporation.

ServiceMaster. (1995). Annual report to the shareholders for 1994. Downer's Grove, IL: ServiceMaster Corporation.

ServiceMaster. (1996). Annual report to the shareholders for 1995. Downer's Grove, IL: ServiceMaster Corporation.

Simmons, R. (1996, December 12). Clunky, comfy Birkies have loyal following. *St. Louis Post-Dispatch*, p. 9.

Skooglund, C. (1994, December). Speech given at Business and Ethics conference in Prague, Czech Republic.

Sloan, A. (1996, January 15). For whom Bell tolls. *Newsweek, 15*, 37.

Sowder, J. (1996, Spring). The 100 percent satisfaction guarantee: Ensuring quality at Hampton Inn. *National Productivity Review*, pp. 53–66.

Sri Guru-Granth Sahib (Vol. I). (Gopal Singh, Trans.). (1960). New York: Taplinger.

Starcher, G. (1995, April). Ethics and entrepreneurship: An oxymoron? Paper presented at European Social Venture Network conference, Tuscany, Italy.

Strohecker, B. (1996, August). A business built on trust. *Guideposts*, pp. 6–9.

The Sunnah. (1975). Chicago: Kazi Publications.

Sunoo, B. P. (1994). Birkenstock braces to fight the competition. *Personnel Journal, 73*(7), 68–75.

Talmud of Babylonia: An American translation. (A. J. Avery-Peck, Trans.). (1995). Atlanta: Scholars Press.

Tart, C. T. (1985). Subtle energies, healing energies. *Interfaces: Linguistics, Psychology, and Health Therapeutics, 12*(1), 3–10.

Tatra: A Detroit rescue. (1993, May 22). *The Economist*, p. 74.

TDIndustries. (1994). *Mission statement*. Dallas: Author.

Telschow, R. (1993, January). Quality begins at home. *Nation's Business*, p. 6.

Thompson, J. W. (1992). Corporate leadership in the twenty-first century. In J. Renesch (ed.), *New traditions in business*. San Francisco: Berrett-Koehler.

Tibetan Dhammapada: Sayings of the Buddha (G. Sparman, Trans., of the Tibetan version of the Udanavarga). (1986). London: Wisdom Publications.

Tichy, N. M., and Sherman, S. (1993). *Control your destiny or someone else will*. New York: Doubleday.

Tom's of Maine. (1995). *Annual Report, 1995*.

Tulin, D. P. (1994, February 22). Letter to the editor. *The Wall Street Journal Europe*, p. 9.

Tully, S. (1991, July 29). Who's who in the East. *Fortune*, pp. 155–160.

Vaill, P. (1989). *Managing as a performing art: New ideas for a world of chaotic change*. San Francisco: Jossey-Bass.

Vogl, A. J. (1993, July/August). Risky work. *Across the Board*, pp. 27–31.

Walton, S. (1992). *Made in America*. New York: Doubleday.

Waterman, R. H. Jr. (1994). *What America does right*. New York: Norton.

Watkins, K. E., & Marsick, V. J. (1993). *Sculpting the learning organization: Lessons in the art and science of systematic change*. San Francisco: Jossey-Bass.

Watson, T. J. Jr. (1990). *Father, son and co.: My life at IBM and beyond*. New York: Doubleday.

Wheeler, M. L. (1995, November). *Diversity: Business rationale and strategies*. New York: The Conference Board.

Wheeler, M. L. (1996, December 9). Diversity: Making the business case. *Business Week*, pp. 89–131.

Whitley, E. (1994, December). Company whose results spell success. *Reader's Digest: British Edition*, pp. 124–129.

Williams, M. (1994, October 25). Some plants tear out long assembly lines, switch to craft work. *The Wall Street Journal Europe, 12*(188), 1, 8.

Yoder, S. K. (1994, September 8). How H-P used tactics of the Japanese to beat them at their game. *The Wall Street Journal Europe, 12*(155), 1, 7.

Young, D. (1994, July 5). We'll do your dirty work. *Chicago Tribune*, p. 1 of Business Section.

Zachary, G. P. (1994). Levi tries to make sure contract plants in Asia treat workers well. *The Wall Street Journal Europe, 12*(127), 1.

The Author

DOROTHY MARCIC recently returned to the United States after living for four years in Prague, where she was a Fulbright Scholar, teaching MBA students and practicing managers at the University of Economics–Prague and the Czechoslovak Management Center. Marcic is currently president of DM Systems, Ltd., and has consulted to AT&T Labs, the U.S. Department of State, Eurotel, the Czech Ministry of Finance, and numerous other organizations.

Marcic's expertise includes working with cross-cultural groups and organizations. During five years of consulting with Bell Labs, she developed a training program called Management of Diversity. She also spearheaded organizational analysis and intervention projects with the Cattaraugus Center, two arts organizations in the Twin Cities, and the Salt River–Pima Indian Tribe in Arizona.

Marcic served as a faculty member for two years at the Autonomous University of Guadalajara, Mexico, and later supervised a summer school in Guatemala. In addition, she served as adviser to the U.S. Ambassador of the Czech Republic and as a delegate to the United Nations Economic and Social Develop Summit in Copenhagen, where she conducted three workshops on ethical management at the Non-Governmental Organization (NGO) Forum. Marcic is the author of *Women and Men in Organizations* (1984), *Management International* (1994), and *Organizational Behavior* (1995).

She lives in Nashville, Tennessee. Her Website is http://www.marcic. com.

Index

Golden Rule, 5–7, 59, 66
Green, F. B., 16
Green Chip companies, 90–91
Greenleaf, R. K., 81
Greig, R., 63

H

Hagemann, H., 65
Hallmark Cards: and family control, 105; and justice, 73–74
Hammer, M., 27, 113
Hampton Inns, virtues at, 129
Handl, M., 136–137
Hansen, M. V., 135
Harbor Sweets, and trust, 51
Hardaker, M., 55
Harley-Davidson, virtues at, 111
Harley Training & Consulting, 107n
Harman, W. W., 21
Hatch, E., 16
Havel, V., 130
Hawley, J., 28
Heider, J., 10
Hendricks, R., 72
Henkoff, R., 90
Herman, S., 58–59
Herzberg, F., 138
Hewlett-Packard: justice at, 98–101; service at, 82; trust at, 52, 100
Hillel, Rabbi, 5
Hinduism: spiritual laws from, 4, 6, 17, 21; and virtues, 50, 77, 82
Hockaday, I., 74
Hofstede, G., 135
Hormann, J., 21, 135
Humility, and service, 81–85
Hurt, J., 78

I

Iacocca, L., 55, 137
IBM: and compensation, 94–95; and unity, 55
Idea Connection Systems: consultation at, 106–107; justice at, 72, 105; respect at, 102–105; service at, 80; spirituality at, 128
Intel, and trust, 93
Intellectual dimension: attributes of, 28–29, 31–32, 33; balance in, 36, 40; and change, 39

International Labor Organization, 22
Islam: spiritual laws from, 7, 37–38; and spirituality, 1; and virtues, 50, 53, 59, 68

J

Jackall, R., 16, 58
Jainism, spiritual laws from, 6
Japan: compensation in, 70; competition from, 56, 100; performance in, 73
Jenkins, H. W., Jr., 99
Jesus, 5, 7, 43
Jirasek, J., 83
Job enrichment, 138
John, 9, 64, 110
Johnson and Sons, S. C., and family control, 105
Judaism, spiritual laws from, 5
Justice: aspects of, 47, 66, 68–76; building, 75–76; and compensation, 68–70; and diversity, 74–75; example of, 98–101; and organizational goals, 121–122; and performance, 73–74; and workforce reduction, 70–73

K

Kanter, R. M., 69, 138
Kerr, S., 117
KFC, service at, 79
King, N., Jr., 83
Knecht, G. B., 85
Kodak, and justice, 72
Koestenbaum, P., 56, 71
Kouzes, J. M., 134–135
Kurtz, E., 137

L

Lao Tsu, 81, 96
Larkin, S., 129
Larkin, T. J., 129
Laurent, A., 81
Lawler, E. E., III, 62
Lawton, R., 114
Leavitt, H. J., 125
Levering, R., 97
Levi Strauss & Co., 22
Lewis, C. S., 133
Liebig, J. E., 43, 49, 57, 97, 98, 115–116
Lipman-Blumen, J., 125

Dorothy Marcic is a frequent keynote speaker in the United States and abroad. Her audiences range from multinational organizations to entrepreneurial corporations. For more information call:

Cosby Speakers Bureau
Washington, D.C.: 703-734-2344
Hong Kong: 011-852-2522-4373
E-Mail: cosbyspkr@aol.com

Managing with the Wisdom of Love
Uncovering Virtue in People and Organizations

Dorothy Marcic

ISBN 0-7879-0173-3

Available at fine bookstores
or
Call 800-956-7739 to order direct